GW00691694

DrawPlus X2
User Guide

How to Contact Us

Our main office
(UK, Europe):

The Software Centre
PO Box 2000, Nottingham, NG11
7GW, UK

Main: (0115) 914 2000

Registration (UK only): (0800) 376 1989

Sales (UK only): (0800) 376 7070

Customer Service/
Technical Support:

http://www.serif.com/support

General Fax: (0115) 914 2020

North American office
(USA, Canada):

The Software Center
13 Columbia Drive, Suite 5,
Amherst NH 03031, USA

Main: (603) 889-8650

Registration: (800) 794-6876

Sales: (800) 55-SERIF or 557-3743

Customer Service/
Technical Support:

http://www.serif.com/support

General Fax: (603) 889-1127

Online

Visit us on the Web at: http://www.serif.com/

International

Please contact your local distributor/dealer. For further details please contact
us at one of our phone numbers above.

Contents

1
Welcome

Welcome to DrawPlus X2

Welcome to **DrawPlus** from **Serif!**

From decorative page elements and logos to full-page illustrations, scale drawings, multi-page publications, and Stopframe or Keyframe animations—DrawPlus X2 does it all. With the power of scalable vector graphics at your command, you'll see the creative possibilities open up right before your eyes! Whether you're a beginner or an expert, you'll find easy-to-use tools you can use right away. With version X2, DrawPlus has broken the price-performance barrier once again!

If you have comments or suggestions—or samples of the work you create with DrawPlus—we'd like to hear from you. For complete contact information, see **How to Contact Us** (at the start of this User Guide).

New Features

- **Keyframe Animation** (p. 185)
  Now perform **Keyframe animation** within DrawPlus! Produce smooth, professional and quick-to-design animations as **Adobe® Flash®** files, all from within the Storyboard tab. The **Easing tab** defines editable envelope profiles for defining the rate of change of an object's transformation and attributes. The **Actions tab** can assign "events" (mouse click, hover over, and many more) and an associated action (e.g., jump to a named URL or animation **marker**); develop directly in **ActionScript** for the more adventurous! Use the Keyframe Camera to pan, zoom, or rotate around your animation's keyframes. Add **sound** and **movies** to any Keyframe animation. Export to **Flash, Flash Lite/i-Mode, screensaver** or a choice of **video** formats {including Serif Transparent Video (STV)}.

- **Great performance**
  Benefit from fast and responsive drawing, lightning quick zooming, and scrolling—all while DrawPlus processes essential background tasks effortlessly. You can even edit your document while complex redraws are occurring! DrawPlus takes full advantage of Multi-core-processor PCs.

- **Ease of use**
  Tool feedback now reports object resize dimensions, rotation angles, text leading/wrap/letterspacing, and changes to Shadow position or QuickShape styles—all in-context as you perform the operation. Can't view nodes and feedback clearly? The **Node Size** and **Feedback Size** can be increased on selection handles, fill/transparency paths, line node segments, and more. **QuickShapes** can now be drawn then edited without Node Tool selection.

- **Resource Management** (p. 218)
  Swap out your already placed bitmaps or text fragments in Drawing mode or any Animation mode from the new **Media tab**; a Keyframe animation's movie or audio clip can also be replaced.

- **Perform Powerful Blends** (p. 224)
  The **Blend Tool** now allows for more powerful blending—adjust number of steps, the transform, and/or attribute profiles (rate of change) via a new context toolbar. Objects can be multiply-blended (to/from other blends) to create truly stunning illustrations.

- **Layer work made easy** (p. 134)
  Each layer entry hosts a hierarchical tree view of associated objects (along with thumbnail previews of each object). The tree view greatly improves the ability to select nested objects, view object ordering and allows more focused object editing. Objects can be **named**—useful when using the new **Find Objects** feature (p. 124). Improve productivity by freezing layers at a user-defined DPI (by rasterization)—layers remain uneditable until "unfrozen". Alternatively, freeze specific layer objects at chosen DPI settings.

- **Curved line drawing** (p. 51)
  The Pen Tool now creates lines in either **Smooth joins** or **Sharp joins** mode. Editing Bezier curve segments with the Pen Tool? Use **Ctrl**-click to edit nodes directly—save time jumping between Pen Tool and Node Tool! Adjust control handles, curves, convert lines to curves by dragging them, and more. **Alt**-key changes smooth corners to sharp corners as you draw.

- **Mesh Fill enhancements** (p. 163)
  Use the **Mesh Fill Tool** for subtle but powerful fading and highlighting on your mesh fills. Move and change the colour of one or more mesh **patches** at the same time, just like individual mesh node control.

- **Rotate Canvas** (p. 41)
  Let your canvas rotate through any angle, just like an artist would do in real-life. Great for artists with tablets, for drawing freeform curves at any orientation, and for getting a different perspective of your drawing!

- **Dynamic Preview** (p. 243)
  Dynamically preview intended export output (JPG, PNG, or any other format) at a given DPI, file format, and number of colours. Create, modify, and delete objects on-screen, safe in the knowledge that edited objects will give a true representation of output—a great time-saver for Web graphics developers.

- **Fill Unclosed Shapes** (p. 57)
  Fill-on-Create allow unclosed shapes to be filled—essential for cartoon drawings where the lines may only be required around certain parts of the shape, but the whole shape should still be filled (imagine drawing a red rose, starting from the outer petals and working inward).

- **Pseudo 3D Projections** (p. 235)
  Project objects isometrically onto Top, Front, or Right planes via a
  Projection toolbar. For more advanced projections, take advantage of
  editable Dimetric, Trimetric, Oblique projections, or even create your
  own **Custom** projection.

- **Instant 3D with on-screen transforms** (p. 233)
  Transform 3D objects with in-situ 3D rotational control and editing.
  Apply awesome multi-coloured **lighting effects** (with directional control),
  along with custom **bevel** and **lathe** effect profiles to create your very own
  unique contours. **Hardware-accelerated rendering** boosts redraw
  performance (hardware dependent).

- Some new useful vector editing tools..

    - **Knife Tool** (p. 116) - cut through objects, leaving them in
      multiple parts, still as vectors.

    - **Erase Tool** (p. 117) - remove areas under a drawn freeform
      line of variable nib width—use on any current selection. Great
      for special effects or simply redefining object boundaries!
      DrawPlus automatically selects the Eraser tool for graphics
      tablet users with erasers on them.

    - **Freeform Paint Tool** (p. 117) - The opposite of the **Erase
      Tool**, the tool "adds to" current vector objects (shapes, text,
      bitmaps)—you can even create complex vector shapes from
      scratch.

- **Text Enhancements** (p. 95)
  DrawPlus now offers the **Frame Text Tool**—great for presenting
  paragraph text in square/rectangular frames. **Bullets and Numbering** and
  adjustable **Tab Stops** are new character attributes for artistic, frame, and
  shape text alike. Use **Spell Checker** to proof your output—check any text
  against an editable user dictionary.

- **View Quality** (p. 39)
  Draw in one of several drawing modes to view objects at optimum quality
  (**Normal** mode), unsmoothed (**Draft**) or as single-pixel outlines
  (**Wireframe**). Benefit from increasing drawing performance with Draft
  and Wireframe, and for Wireframe only, precision alignment and the
  ability to better manipulate overlapping object outlines.

- **How To tab—context-sensitive documentation at your fingertips**
  DrawPlus X2 topics are context-sensitive and are activated by clicking a tool, or by using a tool to perform an action on a selected object. Each topic provides illustrated instructions to show you how to use the tool on the current selection.

- **..and some very useful improvements you've been asking for!!**
  QuickShapes can now be drawn then edited without Node Tool selection. A font's name, typeface and flyout preview now show on the Text context toolbar. Jump between your current and previously used tool with the **spacebar**. A new Pages tab displays your documents' pages as thumbnails for easy page navigation (Drawing mode only). Stopframe animation now uses a redesigned workspace-wide Frames tab—also use object **blending** to create animation Stopframes quickly. Stopframe animations can now have multiple layers too. **Shadow Tool** shows on-the-page control nodes for opacity, blur and shear (X and Y) adjustment. As an aid to document navigation—jump between drawings with single-click document tabs. **Ctrl**-drag over parts of objects will create a multiple selection (without having to encompass entire object area). A new **HSL Slider** mode is added to the Colour tab. The Pointer Tool can now rotate or shear objects. And finally... View in-context resize dimensions, rotation angles, line lengths, and curve segment lengths with **Tool Feedback**.

Established features

- **Multipage Document Support**
  From startup to printout, the versatile DrawPlus engine sustains your creativity. Choose from a wide range of **preset document types**, including **booklets** and folded **documents**. Work on pages right side up... **automatic imposition** assures correct order and orientation of your output. Use DrawPlus's always-at-hand collection of popular design templates (Greeting Cards, Invitations, Letterheads, and more) to create designs quickly.

- **Total Ease-of-Use**
  You'll find accelerated learning tools like ToolTips, and context-sensitive
  Hints & Tips. The tabbed and dockable Studio tabs—storing hundreds of
  preset lines, fills, transparencies, and design elements—is always
  convenient and ready to use. Even collapse, group or resize in any
  combination or direction to maximize your screen area for design. You
  can save your current tab layout as a separate workspace for recall
  whenever you wish. Especially for working at high zoom levels, the
  Navigator tab affords a thumbnail of your entire drawing with the visible
  area shown as a draggable view box. **Context toolbars** host tool options
  and settings that dynamically change according to the currently selected
  object or tool used in your drawing. Only the necessary tool settings and
  options are at hand for edit or reference, speeding up the design process
  while making the user experience easier.

- **QuickShapes**
  QuickShapes work like intelligent clipart… or the most powerful set of
  drawing tools you've ever envisaged. Even extremely complex shapes
  like spirals, stars, and webs are simple to draw and customize using
  QuickShapes. QuickShapes will also take text as with freeform shapes.
  Type directly into any shape! **Shape text** flows to fit the containing object
  for unlimited layout possibilities. Great for flowcharts and family trees!

- **Working with Text**
  Edit shape text or standard (free) text right **on the page...** apply basic
  formatting from the always-at-hand Text context toolbar. Control
  advanced properties like text flow (wrap), kerning, leading, paragraph
  indents, above/below spacing. **Need foreign language support?** Simply
  paste text in Unicode format as either formatted RTF or unformatted plain
  text. **Font substitutions** during the opening of third-party DrawPlus or
  PDF files offers an interactive means of managing missing fonts.

- **Professional-Standard Drawing Features**
  Features like converting **text to curves**, defining custom **envelopes**, fully
  customizable **drop shadows**, layers, and **scalable** vector graphics give
  complete creative power. Plus special commands like Contour for
  outlining and edge effects... Add to composite two shapes into one...
  Subtract for cropping and masking... Intersect to carve out unique shapes
  and regions. With our **Autotrace converter**, bring paint-type art into
  DrawPlus in fully editable vector format.

- **Brushes**
  Unleash the painter within you, with DrawPlus's powerful **Paintbrush Tool** and the supporting Brush tab's galleries! Many vector- and Bitmap-based brush types are at your disposal—pick from charcoal, pastel, pen, pencil and various paint categories, or create your own.

  Using a pressure-sensitive pen tablet? Pressure sensitivity is supported (via a Pressure tab) with preset or custom pressure profiles and control over the maximum and minimum pressure applied. Additionally, scale the brush stroke's width and opacity with pressure. Pressure sensitivity is simulated when applying brush strokes with your mouse.

- **Design Power with Colour Gradient Fills**
  The **Gradient Fill Editor** allows you to adjust gradient contour and tint any portion of the colour spread, locate key colours precisely... and select from RGB, HSL, CMYK, PANTONE® or Registration colours via a Colour Selector.

- **Advanced Fill Support**
  Apply high-end linear, radial, conical, ellipse, three colour, four colour, Square, and Plasma **fills** to any text or shape for exciting, professional results. Simply apply solid colours from the Studio's Colour tab or Swatches tab onto a fill path to add or replace colours for more subtle gradients. Choose colours from different colour mixing modes in the Colour tab—**HSL Wheel**, **HSL Square**, **RGB Sliders**, **CMYK Sliders** or Tinting all offer different ways to mix colour. Load **RGB**, **CMYK** and **co-ordinated "themed" palettes** from within the Swatches tab. Use Bitmap fills for textures and backgrounds. Add, view, edit, or delete colours used in your current drawing from within a saveable **Document Palette**. Even import your own bitmaps and use them as fills on DrawPlus objects! Plus **Mesh Fills** for impressively varied gradients using a path-node network. Define new colour sets based on a base colour—this linkage can transform the drawing's colour scheme instantly, by simply modifying that base colour. Apply a paper texture (**Canvas**, **Cartridge**, **Embossed**, **Parchment**, and **Watercolour**) to layer-specific objects—give a textured look to any artwork. Perfect as a complement to your final composition!

- **Transparency Effects**
  Transparency can make the difference between flat, ordinary visuals and sparkling realism! And DrawPlus provides it all—a full range of transparencies for shading, shadows, reflections, depth effects, and more.

- **Versatile Line Drawing**
  Sketch using **calligraphic lines** with an adjustable pen angle. Add **rounded corners** when and where you need them. Create and save your own line styles by using customizing dot and dash patterns... and choose different end caps and joins.

- **Chain Lines**
  Here's the ultimate in decorative line effects: easy to apply from the scores of pre-supplied choices, just as easy to edit or create from scratch! **Chains** take drawn objects and link them in sequence along a designated line, for marching footprints, themed borders, and much more.

- **Dimension Lines and Scale Setting**
  Click a couple of times to take linear or angular measurements of any object on the page—DrawPlus displays the dimension using your choice of ruler units, at your specified scale (say, one inch to two feet). **Dimensions** update when objects are moved or resized! Design room layouts, make maps, draw scale models... the choice is yours.

- **Connectors**
  For drawing dynamic flow diagrams, schematics, family trees, and organization charts, **connector objects** let you link your boxes and symbols and then rearrange at will. Connection points stay put on each object... keeping connections intact. Auto Connectors intelligently display bridges at line crossings, and even route themselves around obstructive objects.

- **Natural Curve Editing**
  Simply click and drag to break and redraw a curve at any node. Apply smoothing selectively to freeform curves to eliminate that "shaky hand" appearance.

- **Intelligent Curve Tracing**
  Simply "connect the dots" to trace around curved objects and pictures... the Pen Tool features **Smart segments** that use automatic curve-fitting to connect each node!

- **Comprehensive Design Gallery**
  The Gallery tab provides an impressive selection of instantly available Arts&Crafts, Cartoons, ShapeArt, Home design symbols, and various other connecting symbols for family trees, electronics, computers, and many more. Use the Gallery to additionally store and organize your own favourite designs for future use!

- **Picture Import and Adjustments**

  Import pictures from hard disk, CD/DVD, PhotoCD, digital camera or scanner. Use image adjustments for quick fixes (or special effects) such as Red Eye Tool, Auto Levels, Auto Contrast, Brightness/Contrast, Channel Mixer, Colour Balance, Curves, Diffuse Glow, Dust and Scratch Remover, Shadows/Highlights, various blurs.. and many more. Apply adjustments singularly or in combination.

- **Animation Mode**

  Tap the power of QuickShapes to turn out Web **animations** in no time—using advanced features like onion skinning, backgrounds, overlays, and frame management.

- **Web Image Slices, Image Maps, Rollover States**

  Beat the pros at their own game by using these techniques to add links to your Web graphics! With a few clicks, divide images into segments—each with its own hyperlink and popup text—or add hotspots to specific regions. Even let DrawPlus create interactive rollover Web graphics that highlight or change state when users mouse over or click!

- **Web Browser Preview**

  One click lets you see how your graphics will display in a Web browser, so you can quickly check quality, transparency, hyperlinks, and rollover behaviour prior to final export.

- **Filter Effects**

  Drop shadows starting to wear a bit thin? Enliven your text with fully adjustable **Inner Shadow, Glow, Bevel, and Emboss filters...** easy to apply and sure to impress. Apply soft edges with the **Feathering** filter effect—great for blends, montages, vignetted photo borders, and much more.

- **Dramatic Dimensionality**

  Why settle for only two dimensions? **Instant 3D** adds realistic depth to ordinary objects and text. Use one master control panel to vary extrusion, rotation, bevel, lighting, texture, render and more.

- **Astounding 3D Lighting and Surface Effects**

  Advanced algorithms bring flat shapes to life! Choose one or more effects, then vary surface and source light properties. Start with a pattern or a function, adjust parameters for incredible surface contours, textures, fills. The Studio's Effects Tab offers preset 3D effects you can apply and customize as you wish.

- **Perspective Effects**
  Get a new slant on things... With a context toolbar flyout full of presets plus a built-in tool for freeform adjustments, the **Perspective Tool** lets you tilt and skew text (or any other object) for truly "spatial" results!

- **Cropping**
  Any object can serve as a **"cookie cutter"** for trimming one or more other objects into a single shape... and the effect is reversible so you won't lose your originals. Great for creating "reflections" of complex scenes!

- **Roughen Tool**
  For **jagged, jaunty edges** on text, lines, or QuickShapes, just drag the tool up or down for subtle or bold results.

- **Border Wizard**
  Vastly flexible **Border Wizard** instantly adds borders to the page or to individual objects. Choose a border from the extensive library, or be creative and let Border Wizard guide you through building a unique design.

- **Object Default control**
  Set your intended object's default line colour/style, fill, and transparency before even drawing your object! As a more powerful default control, **Synchronize Defaults** lets you adopt a currently selected object's attributes for future objects; For example, select a red brush stroke, to subsequently paint in red, then a green brush stroke to paint in green; all or selected attributes can be affected. Global and object-specific defaults can be reset independently.

- **Image Export Optimizer**
  The **Export Optimizer** lets you see how your image will look (and how much space it will take up) before you save it! Its multi-window display provides side-by-side WYSIWYG previews of image quality at various output settings, so you can make the best choice every time.

- **PDF Export/Import**
  Step up to the worldwide standard for cross-platform, WYSIWYG electronic information delivery. Your **PDF output** will look just like your DrawPlus document... in one compact package with embeddable fonts, easily printable or viewable in a Web browser. Unlock the contents of third-party PDF drawings using DrawPlus's impressive "open PDF" feature—objects can be brought into a new drawing with a single-click for immediate editing.

- **Professional Print Output**
  PDF export to the PDF/X-1 or PDF/X-1a file format is a great choice for professional output from DrawPlus. Deliver with confidence to your print partner, safe in the knowledge that your single composite print-ready PDF drawing includes all fonts and colour information for spot or process colour separation. Select file information, crop marks, registration targets, and densitometer/colour calibration bars for inclusion in your PDF. Spot or process colour (CMYK) separations for full colour printing are possible. You have full control over prepress settings for output.

Registration, Upgrades and Support

If you see the Registration Wizard when you launch DrawPlus, please take a moment to complete the registration process. Follow the simple on-screen instructions and you'll be supplied a personalized registration number in return. If you need technical support please contact us, we aim to provide fast, friendly service and knowledgeable help. There's also a wide range of support information available 24 hours a day on our website at **http://www.serif.com**.

Installation

System Requirements

Minimum:

- Pentium PC with CD-ROM drive and mouse (or other Windows-compatible pointing device)

- Microsoft Windows® 2000, XP, or Vista operating system

- 256MB RAM

- 576MB (recommended full install) free hard disk space

- SVGA display (800x600 resolution, 16-bit colour or higher)

Additional disk resources and memory are required when editing large or complex documents.

 To enjoy the full benefit of brushes and their textures, you must be using a computer whose processor supports SSE. On brush selection, an onscreen message will indicate if your computer is non-SSE.

Recommended:

As above but:

- Dual-processor PC technology

- SVGA display (1024x768 resolution, 16-bit colour or higher)

Optional:

- Windows-compatible printer

- TWAIN-compatible scanner and/or digital camera

- Pressure-sensitive pen tablet (Serif GraphicsPad or equivalent)

- 3D accelerated graphics card with DirectX 9 (or above) or OpenGL support

- Internet account and connection required for accessing online resources

First-time install

To install DrawPlus X2 simply insert the DrawPlus X2 Program CD-ROM into your CD-ROM drive. The AutoRun feature automatically starts the Setup process. (If it doesn't, follow the manual install procedure described below.) Just answer the on-screen questions to install the program.

DrawPlus X2 Resource CD-ROM

If you also have the DrawPlus X2 Resource CD-ROM, it's a good idea to install that as soon as you've finished installing from the DrawPlus X2 Program CD-ROM. Again, the AutoRun feature will automatically start the Setup when the Resource CD-ROM is inserted into your CD-ROM drive.

Manual install/re-install

To re-install the software or to change the installation at a later date, select **Settings/Control Panel** from the Windows Start menu and then click on the **Add/Remove Programs** icon. Make sure the DrawPlus X2 Program CD-ROM is inserted into your CD-ROM drive, click the **Install...** button and then simply follow the on-screen instructions.

First-time install

DrawFiles X2 Resource CD-ROM

Manual installation-install

2

Getting Started

Startup Wizard

Once DrawPlus has been installed, you're ready to start. Setup adds a **Serif DrawPlus X2** item to the **All Programs** submenu of the Windows **start** menu.

- Use the Windows **Start** button to start DrawPlus (or if DrawPlus is already running, choose **New>New from Startup Wizard...** from the File menu) to display the Startup Wizard.

The Startup Wizard offers different routes into the program for you to explore:

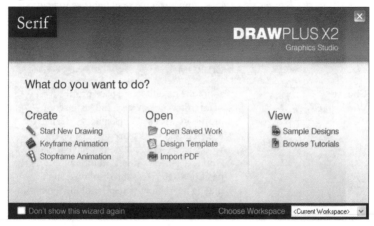

The above options are described as follows:

Create		Allows you to....
	Start New Drawing	create a drawing from scratch
	Keyframe Animation	create a Keyframe animation
	Stopframe Animation	create a Stopframe animation
Open		

	Open Saved Work	open and edit your saved DrawPlus drawings
	Design Template	create an instant drawing or animation from a design (requires DrawPlus X2 Resource CD-ROM)
	Import PDF	import an Acrobat PDF document created from a wide range of applications
View		
	Sample Designs	load some example drawing files to boost your imagination!
	Browse Tutorials	access the DrawPlus tutorials (more available on DrawPlus X2 Resource CD-ROM)
Choose Workspace		adopt the default workspace profile **<Default Workspace>**, the last used profile **<Current Workspace>**, a range of user-focused workspace presets, or a workspace you've previously saved. Each workspace preset stores Studio tab positions, tab sizes, and displayed and hidden tab options. (See Using the toolbars and tabs.)

TIP: To quickly see a new drawing, based on DrawPlus's defaults, select **cancel** in the top-right corner of the Startup Wizard.

Starting with a Design Template

It's so much easier creating drawings with a little bit of help—DrawPlus can utilize a whole range of Design Templates which will speed you through the creation of all types of drawings and animations! Templates can be thought of as "object factories." They let you pick a design and leave you with one or more new objects on the page. If the design is exactly what you want then all that is left is for you to print it or export it. If you want to personalize the design or add to it then you need to know how to work with objects!

 All templates are only available on the DrawPlus X2 Resource CD, which is supplied separately.

To create a drawing from a Design Template:

1. Launch DrawPlus, or choose **New>New from Startup Wizard...** from the File menu. You'll see the Startup Wizard.

2. Select **Open>Design** Template.

3. From the dialog, select a drawing category on the left, and examine the designs on the right. Click the thumbnail that's closest to the one you want, then click **Open**.

The design is loaded and forms the basis of your new **unsaved** drawing or animation. When you make any changes, you'll be prompted to save the drawing or animation to a file name.

 The above method is the only way to access Design Templates. If you've switched the Startup Wizard off (and don't see it when you start up), you can switch it on again. Choose **Options...** from the Tools menu and check **Startup Wizard** from the **Ease of Use** menu option.

Starting with a new drawing

The first time you launch DrawPlus, you'll see the **Startup Wizard**, with a menu of choices. The **Create>Start New Drawing** option offers an easy way to create your new drawing and takes care of the initial setup for the particular type of document you'll be producing.

To start a new <u>drawing</u> from scratch using the Startup Wizard:

1. Start DrawPlus (or choose **File>New>New from Startup Wizard...** if it's already running).

2. Select **Create>Start New Drawing** from the Startup Wizard.

3. Select a document category from the Documents pane (and a sub-category if applicable). Categories contain preset document types or if you select **Regular**, you can choose from standard document sizes presented in Portrait or Landscape sub-categories. For custom sized pages, choose the **Custom Page Setup** button at the bottom of the dialog.

4. Select a document type thumbnail from the right-hand pane and click **Open**. The new document opens.

The **My Templates** category lets you base your new drawing on a previously saved template.

To start a new drawing during your DrawPlus session:

- Click the [ ] **New Drawing** button on the Standard toolbar (if Startup Wizard is disabled).
  OR
  Choose **New>New Drawing** from the File menu.

You'll get a new drawing in a new untitled window each time you choose this method—the default page size is adopted.

You can always adjust the page size and document format later via **File>Page Setup...**.

To turn on/off the Startup Wizard:

1. Choose **Options...** from the Tools menu.

2. Click **Ease of Use** and check/uncheck **Startup Wizard**.

TIP: To start with a new animation, see **Getting started with animation** on p. 173.

Opening a saved document

You can open an existing DrawPlus drawing from the Startup Wizard, Standard toolbar or the File menu. Once open, drawings can be made currently active from a drawing tab or via the Window menu.

To open an existing document from the Startup Wizard:

1. Select Open>Open Saved Work option. In the Documents pane of the Open Saved Work dialog, you'll see either your computer's folder structure for navigation to your DrawPlus drawings (Folders tab) or a list of most recently used drawings (History tab). Preview thumbnails are shown in the adjacent pane.

2. Select a thumbnail from the pane, then click **Open**.

To open an existing document via toolbar or menu:

1. Click the **Open** button on the Standard toolbar, or select **File>Open....**

2. In the Open dialog, navigate to, then select the file name and click the **Open** button.

Displaying drawings

If you open multiple drawings at the same time, you can easily jump between drawings by selecting a drawing name from the Window menu. Unsaved drawings are indicated by an asterisk; the currently active document is shown with a tick.

Alternatively, you can simply click on a open drawing's tab at the top of the workspace to make it active (e.g., the unsaved drawing "Peppers"). Drawings that are not active are greyed out.

Opening PDF documents

It is possible to open any Acrobat PDF document created from a wide range of applications—once opened you can save the PDF file as a DrawPlus Drawing (.DPP) as for any other drawing. The character formatting, layout and images in the original PDF document are preserved to allow for editing of the imported content.

DrawPlus also allows you to publish any DrawPlus drawing as an Acrobat PDF. (See **Publishing as PDF** on p. 248.)

To open an existing PDF from the Startup Wizard:

1. Select the **Open>Import PDF** option.

2. Select a PDF file from the dialog, then click **Open**.

To open a PDF file:

1. Select File>Open....

2. Select the file, and click the **Open** button. The PDF document is loaded and the drawing will repaginate to the number of pages of the original PDF document.

3. Use **Save** or **Save As...** in the File menu to save as a DrawPlus Drawing (*.DPP). The file name is by default based on the original PDF file name but this can be edited as required.

Saving your work

DrawPlus saves its documents as .DPP (Drawing) , .DPX (Template) or .DPA (Animation) files (for Stopframe and Keyframe animation modes).

To save your work:

- Click the 🖫 **Save** button on the Standard toolbar.
  OR
  To save the document under its current name, choose **Save...** from the File menu.
  OR
  To save under a different name, choose **Save As...** from the File menu.

Saving templates

If you've decided that a particular design might be useful in future you can save the layout as a **template**. You can save any DrawPlus drawing as a template (*.DPX) file. When opening a saved template file, DrawPlus automatically opens an untitled copy, leaving the original template intact.

To save a drawing as a template:

1. Choose **Save As...** from the File menu. Under "Save as type:" select the **DrawPlus Template (*.dpx)** option. By default, the template will be saved to a "My Templates" folder so that your templates will be accessible for future use (see **Starting with a new drawing** on p. 21).

2. Enter a file name, leaving the file extension intact, and click **Save**.

To edit a template file directly:

1. Choose **Open...** from the File menu and select **DrawPlus Templates (*.dpx)** in the "Files of type:" box.

2. Navigate to the folder containing your saved template file and select it.

3. To open the original template, uncheck the **Open as untitled** option.

4. Click the **Open** button. You can then make edits to your template.

Undoing/Redoing changes

At this stage, it's worth introducing a quick and easy way of undoing your mistakes! You can reverse any operation on a drawing at any time.

To undo an action:

- Click the **Undo** button on the Standard toolbar.

To redo an action:

- Click the  **Redo** button on the Standard toolbar.

To undo or redo multiple changes with a single action:

- Click the down arrow of the **Undo** or **Redo** button, drag down to highlight the number of actions you wish to undo/redo to, then release the mouse button. This can be used as a repeat function for some actions (e.g., move).

Closing DrawPlus

To close the current document:

- Choose **Close** from the File menu or click the window's ✕ **Close** button.
  OR
  If you have a middle mouse button (wheel), click it when you hover over the document tab at the top of your workspace.

If the document is still unsaved or there are unsaved changes, you'll be prompted to save changes.

To close DrawPlus:

- Choose **Exit** from the File menu.

For each open window, you'll be prompted to save any changes made since the last save.

3

Setting up the document

Setting up a document

A document's page size and orientation settings make a fundamental difference to its layout, and are defined when the new document is first created (see **Starting with a new drawing** on p. 21). If the Startup Wizard is turned off, or you cancel the setup dialog, a new document defaults to A4 (Europe) or Letter size (US) in Drawing Mode. You can adjust the document layout at any time—but as a general rule, it's best to make page setup one of your first creative tasks.

For scale drawings, you can set the ruler units independently of the page measurement units.

To adjust the basic layout of the document (Drawing mode):

1. Choose **Page Setup** from the context toolbar (shown with Pointer or Rotate Tool selected).

2. Select a document category: **Regular**, **Large** (for example, banners or posters), **Small** (for example, business cards), **Booklet**, or **Special Folded**.

   - Where applicable, click in the document list to preview available formats for the selected category. Watch the preview window for an example of each type.

   - If you select Large or Small, you can define a custom document format by clicking **Create Custom...** and entering the desired settings.

   - If you select Regular or Booklet, you can check **Facing Pages** to set up the document using paired, side-by-side pages. This is appropriate if you're creating a document where you need to see both the left-hand (verso) and right-hand (recto) pages, or one that employs double-page spreads where a headline or other element needs to run from the left-hand page to the right-hand page.

3. Select a **Document Size**, set the orientation (Portrait or Landscape) and enter a Width and Height (if a custom setup).
   You can change this later via the Pages context toolbar.

4.   Adjust the document **Margins** to your specifications. You can set the left, right, top, and bottom margins individually, or click the **From Printer** button to derive the page margin settings from the current printer settings. The dialog also provides options for **Balanced** margins (left matching right, top matching bottom) or for two **Mirrored** margins on facing pages where the "left" margin setting becomes the "inside," and the "right" margin becomes the "outside."
    Note: Page margins are represented on the page area by solid blue guides (top, bottom, left and right).

5.   Click **OK** to accept the new dimensions. The updated settings will be applied to the current publication.

The Width and Height of the document (its printing dimensions) are shown in **page units**—for example, inches in Drawing Mode. You can change the unit without altering the document's actual dimensions. The exact method of changing the page unit depends on whether or not you've switched on the **Scale Drawing** option.

To change the page unit:

*   (If the Scale Drawing option is off, as it normally will be) Choose **Options...** from the Tools menu and click **Layout**, then make a selection in the **Ruler Units** box. **Note:** Ruler Units are equivalent to Page Units unless you're working on a scale drawing.

*   (If you've switched on the Scale Drawing option) Choose **Options...** from the Tools menu and click **Drawing Scale**, then make a selection in the **Page Units** box.

Using the page and pasteboard

Most of the DrawPlus display is taken up by a **page** or "artwork" area and a surrounding **pasteboard** area. This arrangement is an electronic equivalent of the system used by traditional graphic designers. They kept design tools and bits of text and graphics on a large pasteboard, and then carefully pasted final arrangements of text and graphics onto a page-sized "artwork" sheet pinned down in the middle of the board.

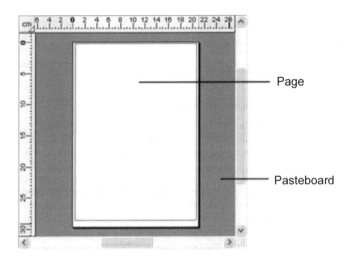

The **page area** is where you put the text and graphic elements that you want to be part of the final output. The **pasteboard area** is where you generally keep any elements that are being prepared or waiting to be positioned on the page area. Your DrawPlus document can include just one page, or many pages. (For details on creating, deleting, and navigating between pages, see **Viewing pages** on p. 38.)

Setting measurement units and drawing scale

If you are trying to create a more complex drawing, or an accurate drawing, or a scale drawing, or just a drawing task that you have to repeat on a regular basis—then you need some organization. You need techniques that allow you to position and draw accurately without effort, and tricks that enable you to organize a drawing so that you can work on one part of it without fear of changing another. And you need to set defaults that save you from having to edit every new object.

We'll look at Rulers, Guides, and Snapping next!

Rulers

The DrawPlus rulers mimic the paste-up artist's T-square, and serve two basic purposes:

- To act as a measuring tool

- To create guides and/or a grid for aligning and snapping

The rulers that surround the page allow you to measure the exact position of an object. Perhaps because they are so obvious and simple, the rulers tend to be ignored—but if you know how to use them they are a powerful tool.

Ruler units

Ruler units used by DrawPlus determine the units displayed on the rulers and the reported units shown when positioning and scaling objects (either around the object or on the Hintline). You can change the ruler units without altering the document's dimensions. Unit settings are saved with your DrawPlus document; as a result loading different documents, templates, etc. may change your working measurement units.

For new documents, the **ruler units** correspond at a 1:1 ratio to the **page units** that define the document's actual printing dimensions (see **Setting up a document** on p. 29). For example, at 100% zoom, one ruler centimetre equals one centimetre on the printed page. As you zoom into your page, you'll see an increasing number of ruler marks appear—allowing for greater drawing accuracy and fine control.

To change the basic measurement unit used by the rulers:

- Choose **Options...** from the Tools menu and click **Layout**, then make a selection in the **Ruler Units** box.

This also lets you set a **Nudge Distance** for moving or resizing objects with the keyboard arrows. You can also force line widths to always be expressed in points.

Drawing scale

You can create **scale drawings** (such as a house plan or model diagram) by setting a ratio other than 1:1 between page units and ruler units. For example, you might wish to set one page inch equivalent to ten (ruler) feet.

 Right-click anywhere on your rulers to quickly swap to a different unit of measurement—the rulers and Transform tab are updated instantly.

To change the drawing scale:

1. Choose **Options...** from the Tools menu and click **Drawing Scale**.

2. Check the **Scale Drawing** box.

3. Use the input boxes to set the drawing scale as a proportion between the
    Page Distance (in **page units** that define the document's actual printing
    dimensions) and the Ruler Distance (in on-screen **ruler units** that
    represent the "real world" objects you're depicting). You can change
    either (or both) units of measurement, or the ratio between them.
    Changing the Ruler Distance automatically updates the **Ruler Units**
    shown on the Layout pane, and vice versa. Once you've made the
    change, ruler markings, dimension lines, and other onscreen units appear
    in the selected ruler units and scaled accordingly onto the page.

Moving rulers

By default, the horizontal ruler lies along the top of the DrawPlus window
and the vertical ruler along the left edge. The default **ruler intersection** is the
top-left corner of the pasteboard area. The default **zero point** (marked as 0 on
each ruler) is the top-left corner of the page area.

To move either ruler to a different position, click and drag on the ruler
intersection button (showing the type of measurement unit).

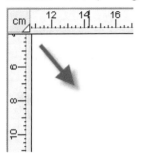

The small tab ⊿ that is shown on the intersection button can be used to set a new ruler origin—simply drag the tab onto the page and release to set the position of your new origin (cross-hair guides and the Hintline toolbar help this positioning). Double-click on the intersection to reset the origin back to its default position. All guide positions are recalculated as the origin changes position.

Double-click on the ruler intersection to make the rulers' zero point jump to the top left-hand corner of the selected object.

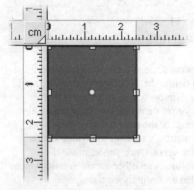

This comes in handy for measuring page objects. If the rulers have already been moved or the object is deselected, double-clicking on the intersection will send the rulers back to the default position.

To lock the rulers and prevent them from being moved, choose **Options...** from the Tools menu, click **Layout**, and check the **Lock Rulers** box.

Hiding the rulers

If you don't need to display the rulers, you can turn them off. Choose **Layout Tools** from the View menu and uncheck **Rulers** on the submenu. Check the item to turn rulers back on.

Rulers as a measuring tool

The most obvious role for rulers is as a measuring tool. As you move the mouse pointer, a small line marker along each ruler displays the current horizontal and vertical cursor position. When you select an object the rulers not only show its position, but also its extent by a lighter coloured area (also showing the object's dimensions).

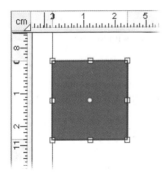

Creating guides

Although rulers are useful for gauging the size and position of objects on the page, they do require you to put some work into positioning objects manually. If you want to position objects repeatedly on the same horizontal or vertical boundary then guides are much easier.

DrawPlus lets you set up horizontal and vertical **guides**—non-printing, red lines you can use to align one object with another. Guides are "sticky" as long as you have **Snap to Guides** turned on (via **Tools>Options>Snapping**), i.e. a moved object will behave as if it is attracted to a guide as you move it close to the line. Guides also attract the object when you are changing its size.

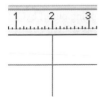

To create a guide:

1. For a horizontal or vertical guide, click on the horizontal or vertical ruler, respectively, at the position you want your guide to appear and hold down the mouse button.

2. Drag onto the page while fine-tuning the guide into its position. A blue line will appear which turns to red after releasing the mouse button. You can use the rulers and Hintline toolbar to ensure your guide is positioned accurately.

> TIP: Hold down the **Alt** key before guide creation to produce a horizontal guide from a vertical ruler and vice versa.

To move, delete and lock guides:

- To move a guide, click and drag it into position with the Pointer Tool.

- To remove a guide, drag and drop it onto the respective ruler.

- To lock the guides and prevent them from being moved, choose **Options...** from the Tools menu, click **Snapping**, and check the **Lock Guides** box.

- To show or hide guides, check or uncheck the **Layout Tools>Guides** option from the View menu.

The blue line that you see around the edges of every page is the margin. You can set the margin size using the command **File>Page Setup...** or in the context toolbar.

The positioning of new guides, and objects that snap to those guides, is influenced by the snapping grid and its settings.

Using snapping

When the global **Snapping** option enabled, and **Snap to Guides** or **Snap to Grid** options checked in **Tools>Options>Snapping**, objects you create, move, or resize will jump to align with nearby, visible guides or a defined grid (of dots, lines, or dashes), respectively. To prevent objects from snapping to guides or grid, uncheck the above options, or switch snapping on/off by checking/unchecking **Snapping** on the Arrange menu.

For snapping to guides, think of an object as being broken into four quadrants such that you drag from the object's upper right quadrant (below) towards the guides to produce the "snapping" effect.

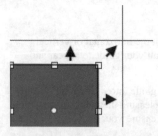

Hiding the guides also hides the margin guides.

To turn snapping on and off:

1. Check or uncheck the **Snapping** item on the Arrange menu.

2. In the Snapping pane, check or uncheck the **Snapping** box.

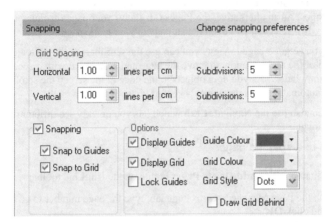

To snap to guides or grid:

*   With the Snapping option checked, check the **Snap to Guides** or **Snap to Grid** option in **Tools>Options>Snapping**.

If you find that snapping is a nuisance because it is stopping you from placing objects exactly where you want them, don't just give in and turn snapping off! Snapping is your best aid in getting objects to fit together when you are assembling a drawing. For example, if you align two objects by eye and then zoom in, you will quickly see that they are not accurately aligned at all!

So if you do find snapping bothersome, it may be that you have the grid spacing set too coarsely to allow you the freedom you need in your design. Go to **Tools>Options>Snapping** to set a finer horizontal and/or vertical grid spacing (you can also change grid colour and style).

To show or hide the snapping grid:

*   Choose **Layout Tools** from the View menu and check or uncheck **Snapping Grid** on the submenu.
    OR
    Choose **Options...** from the Tools menu and click **Snapping**, then check or uncheck the **Display Grid** box.

Viewing pages

DrawPlus provides a variety of ways of getting quickly to the place you need to work. The HintLine toolbar at the bottom of the screen displays the current page number and provides a number of controls to let you navigate around your pages. As an alternative, the **Pages tab** shows your pages as thumbnails, which when selected, will display that page in your workspace.

Once you've got a page in view, you can use the scrollbars at the right and bottom of the main window to move the page and pasteboard with respect to the main window. As you drag objects to the edge of the screen the scrollbars adjust automatically as the object is kept in view.

You can also use the **Navigator tab** which lets you quickly see different parts of the image.

To go to a specific page:

1. Click the ⊞ **Add/Delete Pages** button on the HintLine toolbar.

2. On the Page Manager's **Goto Page** tab, type the page number to go to and click **OK**.

    OR

3. Display the Pages tab (docked at the bottom of your DrawPlus workspace) by clicking the ▬▬ button.

4. Click on a thumbnail to jump directly to that page.

To go to an adjacent page:

- Click the ◄ **Previous Page** or ► **Next Page** button on the HintLine toolbar.

To go to the first page:

- Click the |◄ **First Page** button on the HintLine toolbar.

To go to the last page:

- Click the ►| **Last Page** button on the HintLine toolbar.

Zooming

The Hintline toolbar also allows the user to view and/or edit the page at different levels of detail. You can zoom in/out step-by-step or by a user-defined/preset amount. Panning is also possible.

59% The **Current Zoom** setting on the toolbar displays the current zoom percentage, with 100% representing an actual-size page. Click over the value, then type to enter any zoom percentage up to 5000% or select a preset zoom from the drop-down menu (includes fit to **Full Page** or **Page Width**).

To zoom to a particular view:

- Click ⊖ Zoom Out to decrease the current zoom percentage with each click.

- Click ⊕ Zoom In to increase the current zoom percentage with each click.

- Click the 🔍 **Zoom Tool** and drag out a rectangular marquee on the page to define a region to zoom in to. The zoom percentage adjusts accordingly, fitting the designated region into the window. To zoom out, hold down the **Shift** key when dragging or just right-click on the page. You can also pan around a zoomed-in page while the **Ctrl** key is pressed. To zoom to the current selection, choose **Selection** from the View menu.

- Click the 🖑 **Pan Tool** button to use a hand cursor to click anywhere on the page and drag to reposition the page in the window.

- Click the ▢ **Fit Page** button to adjust the zoom percentage so the entire page area is displayed in the window.

If you're using a wheel mouse, you can scroll the wheel forward or back to move up or down the page, or move horizontally left or right by using the **Shift** key and scrolling together. Try combining the **Ctrl** key and scrolling up or down for immediate in/out zoom control.

View quality

DrawPlus can adopt one of several drawing modes, each one offering different levels of view quality, i.e. **Normal**, **Draft** and **Wireframe**. The respective modes offer decreasing view quality but will produce inversely greater drawing speeds. The difference between modes is especially noticeable on displayed bitmaps, filter effects, and brush strokes. By default,

Normal mode is used for new documents and shows smoothing, Draft shows more sharpness but may leave screen artefacts at different zoom levels, and Wireframe will show just an easily selectable single-pixel outline (without textured strokes, line widths, fills, and 2D/3D effects).

The Draft and Wireframe modes are view modes only, and cannot be output to printer or exported as such.

To change view quality:

• Select **View Quality** from the View menu, then choose **Normal**, **Draft**, or **Wireframe** from the menu.

Adding and deleting pages

DrawPlus uses the **Page Manager** to add one or more pages before or after a currently selected page; you can even make use of an object "cloning" feature which copies objects from a chosen page.

To add one or more new pages:

1. Select a page from which to add page(s) before/after.

2. Choose **Add/Delete Pages** from the context toolbar (shown with Pointer or Rotate Tool selected).
   OR

   Click the 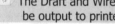 **Add/Delete Pages** button on the HintLine toolbar.
   OR
   Right-click on a page and choose **Insert...** from the Pages tab.

3. On the Page Manager's **Insert Page** tab, specify the following:

   • The number of pages to add

   • The page before (or after) the new pages should be added

   • Whether to duplicate a particular page by copying objects from it

4. Click **OK**.

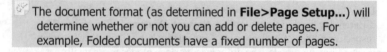
The document format (as determined in **File>Page Setup...**) will determine whether or not you can add or delete pages. For example, Folded documents have a fixed number of pages.

To delete one or more pages:

1. Click the 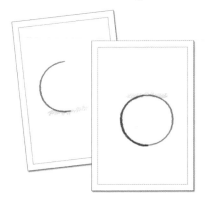 **Add/Delete Pages** button on the HintLine toolbar Choose **Page Manager...** from the Edit menu.

2. On Page Manager's **Delete Page** tab, specify the following:
   - The number of pages to delete
   - The page after which pages should be deleted

3. Click **OK**.

To duplicate a page:

- On the Insert Page tab, you can specify how many pages to add, and where to add them. Check **Copy objects from page** if you want to duplicate a particular page.

Rotating your canvas

Whether you're a user of a graphics tablet or not, dynamically rotating your canvas helps you to maintain natural flow when drawing freeform lines. In particular, freeform curves drawn with Pencil and Paintbrush tools when using the wrist as a pivot benefit greatly from such rotation. If you rotate the canvas by 180° then difficult-to-draw upward curves become easier to draw (becoming downward curves in the rotation process)—taking advantage of the natural arc of the drawing hand.

More practically, if you're relatively new to drawing or a novice graphics tablet user, you'll avoid habits such as trying to physically rotate your tablet!

To rotate your canvas:

Either:

1. Click the ![icon] ▾ **Rotate Canvas** button on the Hintline toolbar (don't click the down arrow).

2. Hover over your workspace until you see the ✋ cursor, then click and drag to rotate the canvas clockwise or counter-clockwise.

3. Once you're happy with the degree of rotation, release the mouse button to reposition the canvas.
   OR

4. Click the down arrow on the ![icon] ▾ **Rotate Canvas** button (Hintline toolbar).

5. Choose a preset angle from the menu (or rotate **To object**; the object is positioned square to the X and Y axes, with the canvas adjusting accordingly).

To reset your canvas:

- With the ![icon] ▾ **Rotate Canvas** button enabled, double-click anywhere on the canvas to reset.

Updating defaults

When you create new objects in DrawPlus, the way they look depends on the current default settings for that particular type of object. DrawPlus stores defaults separately for (1) **lines/shapes** (including **QuickShapes**), (2) **artistic text objects**, (3) **connectors**, (4) **dimension objects** and (5) **brushes**.

Defaults for shape text (as contained in shapes) are distinct from those for artistic text, and are defined along with other shape defaults (they are subsumed under other shape properties). The default line and default fill means the properties of the line or fill type/attributes that will be applied to the next new object you create. Open lines and artistic text objects have separately defined default lines. (Shape text doesn't take a line.)

Initially, the default line is black with a weight of 1.0 pt, the default fill is white and the default text fill is black. For details on manipulating lines and fills, see **Setting line properties** on p. 150 and **Setting fill properties** on p. 145.

Generally speaking, you can set attributes in advance of drawing your intended object. The tabs and context toolbars that support DrawPlus let you pick an attribute, e.g. a line width, colour or style, so that the object you draw will automatically inherit the attributes.

You can use several methods to change the default object settings according to your preferred way or working. Each technique differs depending on the current **Synchronize Defaults** setting on the Standard toolbar, i.e.

- Defaults are changed by **manually** updating to the current object selection, and apply until they are manually updated again. Only use when **Synchronize Defaults** is disabled.

- Defaults are changed **dynamically** by adopting the attributes of the currently selected object. This is possible when **Synchronize Defaults** is enabled (checked).

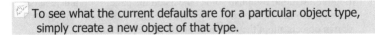

To see what the current defaults are for a particular object type, simply create a new object of that type.

To set object defaults manually:

1. Create a sample object (the object type matching the set of defaults you're updating: line/shape, artistic text object, connector, or dimension object), and alter it to use the specific properties you plan to use as defaults.
   OR
   Use an existing object that already has the right properties.

2. Right-click the object and choose **Update Defaults** (or choose **Update Object Defaults** from the Format menu).

> When you update defaults from a shape, all default shape properties, including **shape text** attributes, are reset at the same time.

> Shape text properties are stored along with other shape defaults, such as line and fill. To avoid altering these settings when updating shape text defaults, create a new sample shape and modify only its text.

Normally, each time you close a document, object default settings are recorded as "master settings" to be used in future documents. To change whether DrawPlus records the defaults as master settings, choose **Tools>Save Settings...** and check the **Object Defaults** box.

To set object defaults dynamically:

1. If disabled, check **Synchronize Defaults** on the ⬚ flyout on the Standard toolbar (enabled by default).

2. Choose **Synchronization Settings...** from the same flyout to optionally select attributes (e.g., Fill colour, Line colour, Transparency, etc) from which new defaults will be made.

3. Begin drawing to establish some objects on the page—continue changing object attributes via the context toolbars or tabs. Note that subsequently drawn objects adopt the attributes of the last selected object.

More about Synchronizing Defaults

The **Synchronize Defaults** feature is particularly useful when you want to quickly inherit the attributes of a currently selected object, e.g. when painting, you might want to reuse the colour of a previously painted brush stroke.

Choosing object attributes

When you select the **Synchronize Settings**, a pop-up dialog lets you check on or off selected attributes which synchronize with, or update to, the currently selected object.

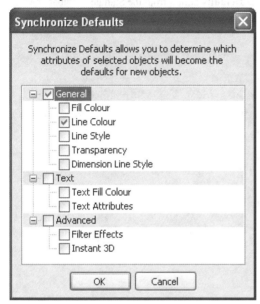

In the above example, only the last selected object's line colour is used for future drawing. If you subsequently change a line colour's attributes, then the defaults will be updated automatically.

Resetting defaults

Two methods for resetting defaults exist—one for a global reset of object defaults and one for resetting only the currently selected object's defaults.

- The global method is useful if you feel the need to get back to basics and reset to DrawPlus's original default settings—a simple click of **Reset Object Defaults** from the **Synchronize Defaults** flyout (Standard toolbar) is all that is needed. This also affects any currently selected objects.

- The reset of current objects method can be used to "revert" selected object attributes back to application defaults. This means that you can localize format control, i.e. the global defaults are not affected. Select the **Reset Current Object Defaults** option from the Standard toolbar directly.

4

Lines, Curves, and Shapes

Selecting one or more objects

Before you can change any object, you need to select it using one of several tools available from the top of the Drawing toolbar (above the creation tools), i.e.

 Pointer Tool
Click to use the **Pointer Tool** to select, move, copy, resize, or rotate objects.

 Rotate Tool
Click to use the **Rotate Tool** to exclusively rotate an object around a centre of origin. You can also use the Rotate Tool to move or copy objects.

 Node Tool
Click to use the **Node Tool** to manipulate the shape of objects, or move or copy objects.

To select an object:

- Click on the object using one of the tools shown above. For the Pointer and Rotate Tools, small "handles" appear around the object indicating selection. For the Node Tool, editable nodes are displayed for lines—sliding handles are shown for adjustment of QuickShapes and text. If objects overlap, click repeatedly (without double-clicking) until the desired object is selected.

 When you draw an object it is initially selected for you so that you can modify it.

Selecting multiple objects

It is also possible to select more than one object, making a **multiple selection** that you can manipulate as if it were one object, or turn into a group object. You can:

- **Position**, **resize**, **rotate**, **shear**, **copy**, **delete**, or **flip** all the objects at the same time.

- **Combine or join** separate objects into new shapes.

- **Align** objects with each other.

- Create a **group object** from the multiple selection (see p. 126), which can then be treated as a single object, with the option of restoring the individual objects later.

To select more than one object (multiple selection):

1. Choose the Pointer, Rotate or Node Tool.

2. Click in a blank area of the page and drag a "marquee" box around the objects you want to select. Dragging with the **Ctrl** key down over only part of your object(s) will include those objects in your selection (great for working at high magnification). To begin the marquee box over a particular object without including that object in the multiple selection, click while pressing the **Alt** key.

3. Release the mouse button. All of the objects within the marquee box are selected and one selection box, with handles, appears around the objects. OR

4. Click on the first object for selection.

5. Press the **Shift** key down then click on a second object.

6. Continue selecting other objects to build up your multiple selection. Handles (or a bounding box, depending on the tool) appear around the multiple selection.

> Selecting multiple objects by either of the above methods produces very different results when objects are to be aligned. See **Aligning and distributing objects** on p. 131.

To select all objects on the page:

- Choose **Select All** from the Edit menu (or **Ctrl+A**).

To add or remove an object from a multiple selection:

- Hold down the **Shift** key and click the object to be added or removed.

To deselect all objects in a multiple selection:

- Click in a blank area of the page.

Selecting overlapping objects

When you have multiple selections where objects overlap the job of selecting a specific one becomes a little more complex. How do you select an object that is "behind" other objects?

To select an overlapped object:

- Repeatedly click with the mouse over the objects. Each time you click at the same location, a different object in the stack is selected, allowing you to select any of the overlapping objects.

Drawing lines and shapes

Lines can be either straight or curved. They have properties like **colour** and **weight** (thickness). When a line (or series of line segments) forms a complete, enclosed outline, it becomes a new **closed** object called a **shape**. Because shapes have an interior region that can be filled (for example, with a solid colour or a bitmap), they have **fill properties** as well as **line properties**.

It's easy to draw straight lines and curves, and connect lines into shapes. Choose one of the line tools shown below from the Drawing toolbar.

 The **Pencil Tool** is used to sketch freeform lines.

 The **Straight Line Tool** is used to draw straight lines, and is hosted on the Drawing toolbar's Line Tools flyout.

 The **Pen Tool** is used to create a series of connected line segments (which may be curved or straight) using a series of "connect the dots" mouse clicks. New line segments are added all the time. The tool is designed for drawing complex, combination curves and shapes in a highly controlled way.

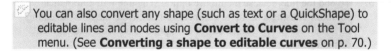

You can also convert any shape (such as text or a QuickShape) to editable lines and nodes using **Convert to Curves** on the Tool menu. (See **Converting a shape to editable curves** on p. 70.)

Lines are drawn using **default line** settings (see **Setting line properties** on p. 150). As soon as you draw a line, or choose one of the line tools when a line is selected, you'll see the line's **nodes** appear. Nodes show the end points of each segment in the line. Curved lines usually have many nodes; straight lines have only two. You can make a shape by extending a line back to its starting point.

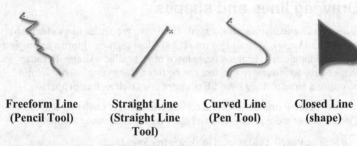

Freeform Line	Straight Line	Curved Line	Closed Line
(Pencil Tool)	(Straight Line	(Pen Tool)	(shape)
	Tool)		

Drawing lines

To draw a freeform line (with the Pencil Tool):

1. Choose the ![pencil] **Pencil Tool** from the Drawing toolbar. Notice that the Pencil context toolbar appears above your workspace when you select this tool.

2. Click once, then drag across the page, drawing a line as you go. The line appears immediately and follows your mouse movements.

3. To end the line, release the mouse button. The line will automatically smooth out using a minimal number of nodes. Note the dots indicating its nodes—at the two ends, and at each point where two line segments come together.

4. (optional) To set the degree of smoothing to be applied to the line (and subsequent lines), set the **Smoothness** value (by entering a value or adjusting the slider) on the context toolbar.

Click its right arrow to display a slider—drag right, then left. You'll see your drawn line—still selected—smooth out (with fewer nodes) as you drag right, and become more jagged (with more nodes) as you drag left. For the smoothest curves the next time you draw a freeform line, leave the sliding arrow towards the left of the slider.

5. To redraw any part of the line, simply click and drag between any two places along it. (The "curve" symbol in the cursor will tell you when you're over the line.) A new freeform line appears, replacing the old line between those two points.

To draw a straight line (with the Straight Line Tool):

1. Click the 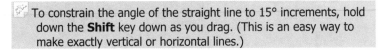 **Straight Line Tool** from the Drawing toolbar's Line Tools flyout. The flyout icon will always reflect the last tool selected.

2. Click where you want the line to start, and drag to another point while holding down the mouse button, then release the mouse button. The straight line appears immediately.

To constrain the angle of the straight line to 15° increments, hold down the **Shift** key down as you drag. (This is an easy way to make exactly vertical or horizontal lines.)

Any kind of open line (that is, one that hasn't been closed to create a shape) can be extended, and you can use any of the three line tools to do so. Use the Pointer Tool and then the line's drawing tool to resize or reshape lines once you've drawn them.

To extend a line:

move the cursor over either of the nodes, a small + cursor will appear. Click at that location.

The line that you drag out will be a continuation of the existing line, as a new line segment.

You can optionally close the curve, creating a new shape that can take a fill!

To draw a curved line (with the Pen Tool):

1. Choose the 🖋 **Pen Tool** from the Drawing toolbar.

2. ⌒ ⌃ From the displayed context toolbar, choose to create your drawn segments in **Smooth joins** or **Sharp joins** creation mode. By default, you'll be in **Smooth joins** mode (i.e., drawing Bézier curves segment-by-segment). Sharp joins would create a zig-zag line without curving through nodes.

3. Click where you want the line to start (**1**).

4. Click again for a new node and drag out a pair of **control handle** which orbit the node (**2**). (Control handles act like "magnets," pulling the curve into shape. The distance between handles determines the depth of the resulting curved line.) Release the mouse button to create your curve segment (**3**).

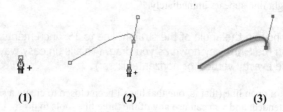

(**1**)   (**2**)   (**3**)

5. To extend an existing line, click beyond the end of your current curve to create a new node (thus creating another curve segment). Normally, curve segments end in a symmetric (evenly rounded) corner (**4**), with control handles locked together.

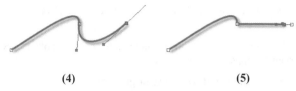

(4)   (5)

6.   However, you can press the **Alt** key while drawing the segment to define a "cusp" or sharp corner (**5**). This locks the control handle on the last created node. For more on line corners, see **Changing nodes and line segments**.

7.   To end the line, press **Esc** or choose a different tool.

Notes

- To select the opposite end node of the curve (i.e., to extend the curve from the other end), press **Tab** before drawing the next segment.

- To constrain control handles to be horizontal or vertical hold down the **Shift** key while dragging.

- To edit the shape of any curve segment without jumping back to the Node Tool, press the **Ctrl** key while clicking a node. You can adjust the line's position and shape by repositioning the selected node or by adjusting the node's control handles.

Drawing shapes

You can make a shape by closing a curve—extending a straight or freeform line back to its starting point. Shapes have an interior which is filled with the current **default fill** (see **Setting fill properties** on p. 145) when the shape is closed.

To close an existing curve (with a straight line):

1. Select the curve with the Node Tool, Pencil or Pen Tool.

2. Click the [icon] **Close Curve** button on the context toolbar. A Straight segment appears, closing the curve.

To close a curve (without new segment):

*   Select the curve with the **Node Tool**, and drag from an end node (note the [cursor] Node cursor), moving the line, onto the other end node (a Close cursor will show); releasing the mouse button will create a shape.

To detach an object's line from its shape:

*   Right-click the object and choose **Detach as New Object>Line**.

> Once detached, the "line" isn't technically a line, nor is it quite the same as a **QuickShape** with a line but no fill. In this case, both the detached line and the formerly filled region become closed shapes with their Line property set to None, but otherwise identical in appearance to the original line and fill.

If you're trying to draw a cartoon outline made up of many independent curves (e.g., a cartoon ear, rose, etc.) you may want fill each curve without closing it. This is made easy by using the **Fill-on-Create** feature.

To fill an unclosed curve automatically:

- Select the Pencil Tool, Pen Tool, or Paintbrush Tool.

- Enable the **Fill-on-Create** button from the context toolbar, and select a suitable fill from the Colour tab. You'll also need to ensure **Select-on-Create** is enabled on the context toolbar (Freehand and Paintbrush tools only).

- Draw a freeform line into a curve. The resulting curve is closed automatically and filled with the current fill colour.

Editing lines and shapes

As objects, lines and shapes are composed of one or more **line segments** (which can be straight or curved) that are joined at their **nodes**. To edit the line or shape, you manipulate its segments and/or nodes, allowing curve redrawing, reshaping (by moving or adding/deleting nodes), and joining two or more lines together.

Redrawing part of a curve

With the **Pencil Tool**, it's easy to redraw any portion of a curve.

To redraw part of a selected curve:

1. Select the line, then the ![pencil icon] **Pencil Tool**. Hover the displayed cursor on the line where you want to begin redrawing. The cursor changes to indicate you can begin drawing.

2. Click on the line, and a new node appears.

3.   Keep the mouse button down and drag to draw a new line section,
     connecting it back to another point on the original line. Again, the cursor
     changes to include a curve when you're close enough to the line to make
     a connection. When you release the mouse button, the original portion is
     replaced by the newly drawn portion.

Reshaping a line

The main tool for editing lines and shapes is the **Node Tool**. In general, you
first use the **Node Tool** to select one or more nodes on the object (**Shift**-click
or drag out a marquee to select multiple nodes), then use the buttons on the
tool's supporting context toolbar. (If some of the bar's buttons are greyed out,
you need to select a node or part of the line or shape to work on.)

Selecting a line or shape with the **Node Tool** reveals its **nodes**. You can
reshape a curved line by dragging or adjusting its nodes or segments.

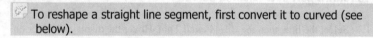

To reshape a straight line segment, first convert it to curved (see
below).

To reshape a curved line:

1.   Click the [▷] **Node Tool** on the Drawing toolbar.

2.   Select any curved line on your page. (Make sure it's a curved line, not a
     straight line.) The line's nodes appear, and the context toolbar also pops
     up.

3. Hover over a segment and drag the segment to form a new curve shape. OR

   Hover over a node (the ✎ cursor will be shown) and click to select the node. Optionally, **Shift**-click or drag out a marquee to select multiple nodes.

   Control handles for the adjacent line segment(s) will appear. Note that each segment in the line has a control handle at either end, so when you select an **end node** or **interior node**, indicated below, you'll see either a control handle on each selected end node (one segment) or a pair of handles at a selected interior node (two segments), respectively, i.e.

4. Drag any selected node to reshape adjacent segment(s). All selected nodes move in the same direction, so you can reshape the curve in complex ways by selecting specific nodes. **Shift**-drag to constrain the movement to horizontal or vertical.

5. Drag one or more control handles to produce very precise changes in the curvature of the line on either side of a node. You can shorten or lengthen the handles, which changes the depth of the **curve** (that is, how far out the curve extends), or alter the handle angle, which changes the curve's **slope**.

TIP: When using the Pen Tool, pressing the **Ctrl** key while clicking a node lets you edit the curve directly. This saves having to jump back to the Node Tool. You can't edit multiple nodes simultaneously.

By **changing the type of node** you can change how the adjacent segments behave.

As a shortcut when selecting nodes, you can press **Tab** or **Shift-Tab** to select the next or previous node along the line (following the order in which nodes were created).

Simplifying or enhancing a line

The more nodes there are on a line or shape, the more control over its shape you have. The fewer nodes there are, the simpler (smoother) the line or shape. You can adjust the **Smoothness** to refine the curve most recently drawn (as long as the line is still selected). It is also possible to add or delete nodes to simplify or enhance curves, and even clean curves (removing unnecessary nodes automatically).

To adjust the smoothness of the most recent pencil line:

1. Choose the [✎] **Pencil Tool** and draw a freeform line.

2. Click the right arrow on the **Smoothness** option and drag the displayed slider left to increase the number of nodes (you can also add absolute values into the input box).

3. To make the curve less complex, i.e. smoother, drag the slider right to decrease the number of nodes.

To add or delete a node:

- To **add a node**, click along a line segment with the Node Tool or Pen Tool to add a new node at that point. The new node will be created and, following a further click, will be selected (complete with attractor nodes as necessary).

- To **delete a node**, select the line with the Node Tool then the node itself and click the **Delete Node** button on the context toolbar (or press the **Delete** key). The node will be deleted, along with any associated attractor nodes, and the line or shape will jump to its new shape. With the Pen Tool selected, you can also delete a selected node by clicking on it.

You can also use the Node Tool to reposition the nodes, and reshape the line or shape, by dragging on the new handles.

To clean curves:

The **Clean Curves** feature automatically removes unwanted nodes present in your drawn curves. The curve shape remains unaltered (compared to smoothness adjustment) but less nodes makes editing more easy.

1.   With the Node Tool, select the curve.

2.   From the context toolbar, choose **Clean Curves**. While still enabled, click the drop-down button to use a slider which controls the extent to which unwanted nodes are removed.

Changing nodes and line segments

Each segment in a line has a control handle at either end, so at each interior or "corner" node (where two segments join) you'll see a pair of handles. The behaviour of these handles—and thus the curvature of the segments to either side—depends on whether the node is set to be **sharp**, **smooth**, **symmetric**, or **smart**. You can quickly identify a node's type by selecting it and seeing which button is selected in the displayed context toolbar. Each type's control handles behave differently as illustrated below.

To change one or more nodes to a different type:

1.   Select the object with the **Node Tool**, followed by the node you want to change (**Shift**-click or drag out a marquee to select multiple nodes).

2.   Click one of the node buttons (described below) on the displayed context toolbar.

 A **Sharp Corner** means that the line segments to either side of the node are completely independent so that the corner can be quite pointed.

 A **Smooth Corner** means that the slope of the line is the same on both sides of the node, but the depth of the two joined segments can be different.

At a **Symmetric Corner**, nodes join line segments with the same slope and depth on both sides of the node.
Note: Normally, **Custom segments** you draw with the Pen Tool end in a symmetric corner.

Smart Corner nodes automatically determine slope and depth for a rounded, best-fitting curve. If you attempt to adjust a smart corner's handles, it reverts to a symmetric corner. You can always reset the node to smart—but to maintain smart nodes, be careful what you click on!

You can also use the context toolbar to define a line segment as either straight or curved.

To change a line segment from straight to curved, or vice versa:

1. With the **Node Tool**, select the leading node of the line segment (the node nearer the start of the line).

2. Then, either:

   - To make a line segment straight, click ![Straighten Line] **Straighten Line** on the context toolbar. The selected segment immediately jumps to a straight line.
     OR

   - To make a line segment curved, click one of the node buttons on the context toolbar: **Sharp Corner**, **Smooth Corner**, **Symmetric Corner**, or **Smart Corner**. You can then adjust the curvature of the newly created curved segment.

To convert to straight lines:

1. With the Node Tool, select the curve.

2. From the context toolbar, choose ![Convert to Straight Lines] **Convert to Straight Lines**. The curve segments are replaced by straight line segments throughout the line.

Adjusting a shape

As described on p. 55, you can easily turn a curve into a shape by connecting its end nodes. You can go the other way, too—break open a shape in order to add one or more line segments.

To break open a line or shape:

1. With the **Node Tool**, select the node on the closed curve where you want the break to occur.

2. Click the ⊢→⊣ **Break Curve** button on the context toolbar so that the line will separate. A shape will become a line, with the selected node split into two nodes, one at each end of the new line.

3. You can now use the Node Tool to reposition the nodes and reshape the line by dragging on the handles.

> When you first break a curve the two nodes are in exactly the same location and so the curve may still look as if it is connected. If you drag one of the red node ends away you will quickly see the separation.

Joining lines together

You can connect any two straight or curved lines to form a new line.

To join two lines together:

1. Select both lines by **Shift**-clicking with any selection tool.

2. Choose **Join Curves** from the Tools menu. The end control node of one line is connected with the start control node of the other.

For other combinatorial effects you can achieve with DrawPlus, see **Combining, cropping, and joining objects** on p. 128.

Using QuickShapes

QuickShapes are pre-designed objects that you can instantly add to your page, then adjust and vary using **control handles**. QuickShapes are added from a flyout containing a wide variety of commonly used shapes, including boxes, arrows, hearts, spirals and other useful symbols.

Once you've drawn your QuickShape, you can adjust its properties—for example, apply solid, gradient or Bitmap fills (including your own bitmap pictures!) or apply transparency effects. You can even use sliding handles to create variations on the original QuickShape.

It's also possible to use the always-at-hand QuickShape context toolbar situated above the workspace to swap QuickShapes, and adjust a QuickShape's line weight, colour, style, and more.

To create a QuickShape:

1. Click the **QuickShape** button on the Drawing toolbar and select a shape from the flyout. The button takes on the icon of the shape you selected.

2. At your chosen cursor position, either:

    *   Double-click to place a default-sized QuickShape.
        OR

    *   Click and drag on the page to draw out your QuickShape to be of a chosen size.

3. New QuickShapes adopt the currently set line and fill in DrawPlus. To constrain the aspect ratio (for example, to obtain a square or circle), hold down the **Ctrl** key while dragging.

All QuickShapes can be **positioned**, **resized**, **rotated**, and **filled**. What's more, you can adjust their designs from within the QuickShape Tool (or **Node Tool**). Each shape changes in a logical way to allow its exact appearance to be altered. The ability to alter the appearance of QuickShape objects makes them more flexible and convenient than clipart pictures with similar designs.

To adjust the appearance of a QuickShape:

1. Click on the QuickShape to reveal sliding handles around the shape. These are distinct from the "inner" selection handles. Different QuickShapes have different handles.

2. Drag the handle To change the appearance of a QuickShape, drag its handles.

For example, by dragging the top sliding handle to the right on the pentagon below will quickly produce an octagon:

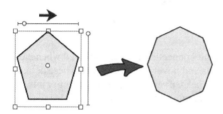

You can also use the Line tab and Swatches tab to alter any object's line/fill properties after it's been drawn.

To reset line and fill defaults for shapes (including QuickShapes):

See **Updating defaults** on p. 43.

Working with connectors

Connectors are special lines that you can anchor to objects, where they remain attached even if one or both objects are moved or resized. Using connectors, you can easily create dynamic diagrams and charts that show relationships, such as family trees, organization charts, and flow charts. If you need to rearrange the elements, the connections are preserved.

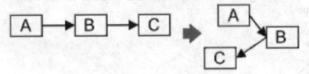

Each DrawPlus object has default connection points, displayed whenever you select one of the Connector tools and hover over the object. These default points (which can't be moved or deleted) are called **Auto Select** points. You can create your own additional **custom** connection points, created with the **Connection Point Tool**, which can be placed anywhere on an object.

The Connector Tool, when selected, offers various types of connector tool on the Connectors context toolbar situated above the workspace. The context toolbar also adjusts a connector's line weight, line end, colour and style.

To create a connection:

1. Select the Connector Tool on the Line Tools flyout (Drawing toolbar). Hover over an object so that default **Auto Select connection points** become visible, e.g. as on the left Quick Rectangle:

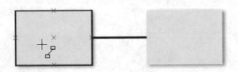

2. From the displayed context toolbar, select the Direct Connector Tool option.

3. Click the connection point on the right edge midpoint of the left shape. Drag to the right and release the mouse button when the pointer is over the connection point on the left edge midpoint of the right shape. (You'll see a box appear around the point when a connection is imminent.) A direct connector will appear between the two connection points.

4. Select the right-hand shape and drag to a new position with the Pointer Tool; the connection points vanish, but the connector remains. The connector follows!

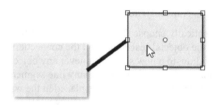

Connector types

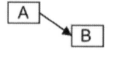

Choose the ⬛ **Direct Connector Tool** option to draw a single, straight-line connector between any two connection points.

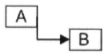

Choose the ⬛ **Right Angle Connector Tool** option for a connector with only vertical and horizontal segments (the connector shape is made up of right angles)—for example, if you're creating a flow chart, organization chart, or tree diagram.

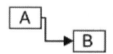

Choose the ⬛ **Auto Connector Tool** option for an adaptable connector that intelligently adjusts its shape to route around "obstructive"

objects. Unlike the other connectors, Auto connectors automatically form "bridges" when crossing each other, so they're perfect for complex diagrams with interwoven pathways.

Using Auto Connectors

By default, new closed objects are **obstructive**—that is, Auto connectors route themselves around the object. New open curves and lines are unobstructive—Auto connectors route across the object. If you wish, you can change this property for a given object.

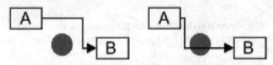

   Obstructive object   **Non-obstructive object**

Auto connectors will automatically choose the best route for a particular path between connectors, given the objects' placement and the connection points you've chosen. They will redraw to a new shape whenever any objects are moved or resized. The shape it assumes will use as many line segments as necessary and will even route around objects that are placed in the way of the original connector. They use horizontal and vertical line segments only.

To Auto Connect between connection points:

1. Draw two objects.

2. Click the **Connector Tool** on the Line Tools flyout (Drawing toolbar).

3. Select the **Auto Connector Tool** option (context toolbar). Default connection points will appear when hovering over any object.

4. Hover over a connection point and drag to another connection point, typically on a different object. Release when the small box appears, and the connector re-anchors.

> Remember that you can change your Direct or Right Angle connectors to be Auto Connectors at any time if you are not happy with your connector positioning.

See DrawPlus help for information about how to route across particular objects.

What if you want to anchor a connector to a specific (custom) point on an object, but it's not one of the default Auto Select connection points? That's where the Connection Point Tool option comes in handy.

To add a custom connection point:

1. Click the **Connector Tool** on the Line Tools flyout (Drawing toolbar).

2. Select the **Connection Point Tool** on the context toolbar. The Auto Select connection points appear in red on a selected object.

3. Click somewhere in the interior of the shape and a blue custom connection point appears. You can add custom connection points anywhere but typically you will want them positioned around the perimeter of an object—to do this hold the **Ctrl** key down when you click.

You can select and move custom connection points with the Connection Point tool. To delete one, simply select it and press Delete. Otherwise, they function basically like default Auto Select connection points, i.e. they can be connected to identically.

Editing connection points and connectors

- To **move** a custom connection point, drag it with the **Connection Point Tool**. You can select multiple points to be moved by **Shift**-clicking or drawing a marquee around the points. To "snap" a connection point to the nearest edge of an object, hold the **Ctrl** key down when you drag the node.

- To **delete** a custom connection point you've added, select it and press **Delete**. Default nodes are fixed and can't be deleted. You can select multiple points for deletion by **Shift**-clicking or drawing a marquee around the points.

- To **move, reshape,** or **detach/reattach** a connector, use the [⟍] **Node Tool** to drag individual nodes. Drag the end node of a connector to detach or reattach it. Changing a connector's shape converts it to a **Custom connector**, losing its Auto properties so you may need to adjust the route to avoid other objects. (See **Editing lines and shapes** on p. 57.) Unlike standard lines, you cannot resize or rotate connectors.

- To **convert** a connector from one type to another, right-click the connector and choose **Connectors**, then select the desired type.

- To edit connector properties like thickness, colour, and line ending, use the standard controls on the Studio's Line tab, Colour tab and Swatches tab just like you would for a standard line.

Converting a shape to editable curves

Now that you know how to **edit a curve**, you may wonder how you can do the same things to a QuickShape, or to text for that matter. The problem is that the Node Tool affects a QuickShape or text object quite differently from the way it edits curves. However, converting QuickShapes to curves provides you with a starting point for your own shapes whereas converting text to curves is one way of incorporating letter shapes into designs.

To convert an object into curves:

1. Select your QuickShape or text object.

2. Choose **Convert to Curves** from the Tools menu. The object is now editable when selected by the Node Tool.

3. Edit the curve outline using the Node Tool.

However they were created, all converted objects behave in a similar manner. For example, you can create some text with the Artistic Text Tool, convert it to curves, then use the Node Tool to edit the curves that make up the letters, just as if you had drawn the letter shapes by hand using the line tools.

 The conversion process loses all of its special properties inherent in QuickShapes and text.

Check **Clean Curves** in **Tools>Options>General** to automatically reduce the number of nodes during convert to curve operations—this makes editing a little easier!

Applying envelopes

An envelope distortion is one that you can apply to any object to change its shape without having to edit its nodes. To understand how an envelope affects the shape of an object, imagine it drawn on a rectangular rubber sheet which is stretched to the outline of the selected envelope. As you might expect, this is a very powerful feature for special effects—and not only for text. For example, you can use envelopes to bend text into a wave, arch, trapezoid, or just about any other shape. You can edit envelopes into custom shapes and apply them to other objects for corresponding effects.

You can use either the **Envelope Wizard** (Tools menu) or the **Envelope Tool** (Drawing toolbar). When the latter is selected, an object's nodes can be moved in order to create custom envelopes or to allow preset envelopes to be applied to the selected object. The displayed context toolbar, shown while the tool is active, offers various options to customize the envelope—envelope shape, line colour, weight, and style can all be altered. It also lets you pick from a range of pre-defined envelopes of various shapes, remove the selected object's envelope or apply curve adjustments on the envelope's boundary.

To apply a preset envelope via Envelope Wizard:

1. Select the object(s) you want to be enveloped.

2. Choose **Envelope Wizard** from the Tools menu. As the first step, the Wizard gives you the choice of applying the distortion either to the currently selected object or to some new text. The next step lets you browse through the possible envelope shapes and preview their effect.

To apply an envelope via the Envelope Tool:

1. Select the object(s) you want to be enveloped.

2. Click the ⊠ **Envelope** button on the Drawing toolbar. Select an envelope preset from the **Preset Envelopes** flyout on the displayed Envelope context toolbar. The first item, User Defined envelope, retrieves the last drawn custom envelope shape (see below) used in your current DrawPlus session.

When you apply an envelope to an object or multiple selection, a single-envelope object is created. This object behaves like a group object, allowing most normal object operations.

To remove an envelope:

- Select the envelope with the **Envelope Tool**, then choose **Remove Envelope** from the Envelope context toolbar.

To create/edit your own envelope:

You can create an envelope or edit any of the preset envelopes once they have been applied by dragging the nodes and handles accordingly.

- Select the object(s) with the **Envelope Tool**. DrawPlus automatically selects the Node tool when an envelope is applied. The Node Tool along with the displayed curve buttons on the Envelope context toolbar lets you reshape the envelope by dragging its corner nodes and attractor nodes, as when editing curved lines. (To review these concepts, see **Editing lines and shapes** on p. 57.) The only difference is that you cannot add or delete corner nodes to an envelope. Envelopes always have exactly four line segments, one on each side.

Applying perspective

The **Perspective Tool**, like the adjacent **Envelope Tool**, produces an overall shape distortion. But while the Envelope effect stretches the object as if it were printed on a rubber sheet, Perspective gives you the visual impression of a flat surface being tilted in space, with an exaggerated front/back size differential. Using the Node Tool, you can achieve just about any freeform viewpoint, making this a versatile effect for both text and shapes.

To apply a perspective effect:

1. Select an object and click the ⬛ **Perspective Tool** button on the Drawing toolbar. The Node tool becomes the active tool and an adjustment slider appears above the object.

2. Either:

*   Drag the ⬧ "3D" cursor over the selected object or drag the special adjustment slider handle left or right to see it respond by tilting in all sorts of orientations. Use Undo if you're not happy with a particular adjustment.
    OR

*   From the context toolbar, select an item from **Perspective Presets** flyout closest to the effect you're after. The first item, **User Defined perspective**, retrieves the last drawn custom perspective shape used in your current DrawPlus session. You can still use the cursor and handles for adjusting perspective.

Using the Gallery

The Studio's Gallery tab serves as a container for a vast array of pre-built design objects and elements you'd like to reuse in different drawings. Arts and Crafts, Cartoons, Connecting Symbols (for family trees, electronics, and computers), Layout Symbols (for garden and home), and ShapeArt are all folders under which various categories (or further sub-folders) are stored. When you install the Draw*Plus X2 Resource CD* the gallery tab also includes further categories (Curriculum and Business) for your use.

The Gallery tab has two parts: (1) an upper **Folder/Categories** drop-down menu and (2) a lower **Designs** window where you can select and drag a design onto your page. The window shows a list of thumbnails representing the designs in the selected category. In this case, a "Smilies" category stored in the Arts & Crafts folder.

The Gallery tab also lets you store your own designs (e.g., room layouts) in the **My Designs** section if you would like to reuse them—the design is made available in any DrawPlus document. You can add and delete your items within each category, with the option of naming elements to facilitate rapid retrieval. You can even create your own design folders and categories if you want to arrange a collection of your own designs (as shown on the next page).

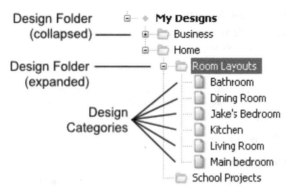

New Design Categories can be added to any Design Folder which exists under the user's **My Designs** category (but not under any read-only pre-defined category). You can rename or delete any design by right-clicking on the design thumbnail.

To use a design from the Gallery:

• Drag any preset design directly onto the page. The Gallery retains a copy of the design until you expressly delete it. You can modify, then drag the design back into your own custom category.

To view your Gallery:

• Click the Studio's **Gallery** tab.

• Select a folder or category from the drop-down menu. The items from the folder's first listed category are displayed by default.

To add, delete, or rename design folders:

1. Right-click in the drop-down menu and choose Add Folder..., Delete Category/Folder, or Rename Category/Folder....

2. For adding and renaming, use the dialog to enter and/or confirm your change.

To add, delete, or rename design categories:

1. Right-click in the Categories list and choose Add Category..., Delete Category/Folder, or Rename Category/Folder....

2. For adding and renaming, use the dialog to enter and/or confirm your change.

To copy an object into the Gallery:

1. Display the Gallery tab's **My Designs** category (or sub-category of that) where you want to store the copy.

2. Drag the object from the page and drop it onto the gallery.

3. You'll be prompted to type a name for the design. (You can name or rename the design later, if you wish.) By default, unnamed designs are labelled as "Untitled."

4. A thumbnail of the design appears in the gallery, labelled with its name.

To delete a design from the Gallery:

- Right-click its gallery thumbnail and choose **Delete Design...** from the submenu.

To rename a design:

- Right-click its thumbnail and choose **Rename Design...**. Type the new name and click **OK**. The new name appears immediately in the gallery list.

5

Brushes

Getting started with brushes

DrawPlus supports vector and bitmap-warped brushes, the former capable of producing scalable crisp brush strokes, the latter producing natural media effects (charcoal, pastel, pen, pencil and various paint effects).

An impressive selection of categorized brush presets can be chosen from the Brushes tab. Each preset can be edited to your own brush design or copied to a newly created name and category. If you'd like complete control over your brush design, new brushes can be created from scratch.

It's perfectly possible to use any DrawPlus vector object or Bitmap graphic to form the basis of a new brush.

Brush strokes can be applied directly to the page from your mouse or tablet with the latter method ideally suited for applying customizable pressure-sensitive strokes to your drawing. However, painting with the mouse still provides a viable alternative to the tablet. Pressure sensitivity is simulated by use of ready-made customizable pressure profile presets.

Another great benefit of DrawPlus brushes is that there's little chance of spilling paint down yourself and you won't need to clean any brushes afterwards! Let's move on to look at painting and brush use.

How do you paint?

Painting in DrawPlus inherits the principles of **Drawing lines and shapes** (see p. 51). The drawing freedom of the Pencil Tool is adapted for brushwork using the dedicated **Paintbrush Tool**. Brush defaults are stored independently of Pencil tool defaults.

You can pick up colour for your brushes as you would for other object, by simply selecting the Paintbrush Tool, choosing your brush type and picking a brush colour from the Colour or Swatches tab.

Using a pen tablet

You can either draw with your mouse or, for a more natural experience, use a pen tablet (e.g., Serif GraphicsPad or equivalent). A pen tablet is comprised of an intelligent electronic pad equipped with a pressure-sensitive pen. A rectangular "active" area responds to pressure applied by the pen.

The pad, when connected to your computer, allows realtime drawing within DrawPlus, making the drawing experience as close to a paintbrush as you can get. The tablet's pressure-sensitive pen tip along with DrawPlus itself allows control of stroke width or transparency when painting or drawing. (see **Pressure sensitivity** on p. 89).

Inspired by a small printed photo or picture? Place the photo directly on top of the tablet and trace its outline(s) with the tablet pen. With the outline(s) stored on a separate layer you can confidently start to paint in the details of another masterpiece!

Using Brushes

The Brushes tab lets you view brushes currently being used in your document as well as serving as a container for supplied brush presets and your own brush designs. It is possible to edit the existing presets and save your customized brush under a new brush name—even store your own brushes under your own categories if you'd like to reuse them in different drawings.

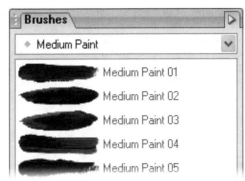

Once you've added your own brush to a category it becomes available in any drawing—simply open the category again, select the brush and paint!

Brush Types

All brushes available from the Brushes tab fall in one of two camps:

- **Stretching**: A standard non-repeating brush where the body is stretched along the length of the brush's body.

- **Repeating**: A repeating brush, as its name suggests, repeats a portion of the brush body over a configurable number of times.

See **Editing brushes** (p. 85) to see how you edit or copy stretching or repeating brushes. To create custom brushes, see DrawPlus Help.

Using Categories

To make sense of all the brush types
available to the user, the preset brushes
are stored under a series of pre-defined
categories under the name **Global**—the
brushes are available to all DrawPlus
documents currently open.

The category names reflect the physical characteristics of the stored brush
texture. You can add, rename and reorder any category and even create nested
categories within categories.

The **Document** category shows the brush types currently in use in the
DrawPlus drawing and is used to "bookmark" brushes for easy reuse in the
future.

If you open a friend or colleague's DrawPlus file which contains some very
appealing custom brushes, you can always "acquire" them by copying them
from the Document category to your own Global category. (See Editing
brushes on p. 85).

To add, rename or delete Gallery categories:

1. Select the category under which you want to add a new category name.

2. Right-click in the Categories list and choose **Add...**, **Rename...** or
    Delete.

3. For adding and renaming, use the dialog to enter your new category
    name.

Selecting brushes

Brush types are hosted as rectangular thumbnail strips in each category of the
Brushes tab. Each thumbnail is supported by descriptive text.

Applying brush strokes

Using the Paintbrush Tool

The [icon] **Paintbrush Tool** is used exclusively to apply brush strokes to the page. The tool is used in conjunction with the Brushes tab.

Before going any further it's worth considering how you plan to paint. Like any project a little planning goes a long way!

There are many ways in which people choose to paint, depending on the subject matter, brush type, and the stage of the painting process. The first concern is which brush type, width, and colour will be adopted on application of your first and subsequent brush strokes.

By the way, the displayed [icon] Brush cursor indicates that the Paintbrush Tool is selected and that you're ready to Paint!

To apply a brush stroke:

1. Select the [icon] **Paintbrush Tool** from the Drawing toolbar.

2. Display the Brushes tab and choose a brush from a category.

3. You can either:

   - Select a Brush width from the **Line** tab, a brush colour from the **Colour** or **Swatches** tab and finally a level of brush transparency from the Transparency tab.
   OR

   - Select a **Colour**, **Width**, or **Opacity** from the Brush context toolbar.

4. Adjust settings such as Smoothness (sets how smooth your stroke is applied) via a slider or click **Fill-on-Create** to fill the unclosed curve produced with the brush stroke with a default fill colour.

5. With the brush cursor drag a brush stroke across your page.

The currently displayed settings in the Brush context toolbar (above your workspace) will be adopted for all brush strokes.

After this first brush stroke, there are two ways in which you are likely to paint subsequently, depending on the extent to which you plan to edit brush strokes as you go. To assist you, the **Select on Create** button on the Brushes context toolbar can be used:

- **Edit then Paint**. With the button disabled, the brush stroke is laid down and is immediately deselected. The stroke needs to be reselected to perform any editing. Use when you're happy to set all the brush properties (colour, brush type, width, etc) before painting (as above), especially if you intend to paint repeatedly with the same brush stroke.

- **Paint and Edit**. With the button enabled, a painted brush stroke will remain selected, meaning that the brush stroke can be fine-tuned via the context toolbar immediately. Use when changing your brush properties frequently, e.g. when adjusting a brush stroke's colour, width, opacity or shape (see **Setting brush properties** on p. 87). The **ESC** key deselects the current brush stroke.

DrawPlus's flexibility still let's you paint and edit without restriction but it's important to know the distinction between the enabled and disabled Select on Create button.

 Trouble applying colour to brush strokes? Remember to select the line swatch on the **Colour** tab.

Setting Brush Defaults

See **Updating defaults** on p. 43.

Editing brush strokes

Any brush stroke laid down can be edited with the supporting dynamic Brushes context toolbar which pops up whenever the Paintbrush Tool is selected. From the context toolbar you can alter the width, colour, opacity and smoothness of the brush stroke amongst others. Fill-on-Create fills the unclosed curve produced by a brush stroke with a default fill colour.

As mentioned at the beginning of the chapter, a brush stroke possesses very similar characteristics to a plain line. Therefore, it's not surprising that any brush stroke can be edited, extended or redrawn with the **Node Tool** (Drawing toolbar) just as for a straight or curved line (see **Editing lines and shapes** on p. 57). The brush stroke path can also be closed or opened.

As a reminder, the selected brush stroke will display it's nodes and segments when the Node Tool is selected. Single or multiple nodes can be deleted, added or dragged around to reshape the brush stroke. You can also fine-tune the brush stroke by dragging the node's control handles as well as changing the node corner type (Straight, Sharp, Smooth, or Symmetric).

> TIP: Use the 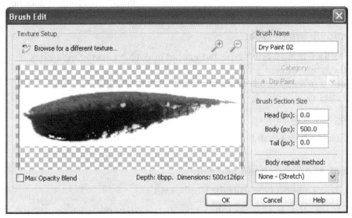 **Reverse Curve** button on the Node Tool's context toolbar to reverse the direction of a brush stroke.

As well as editing brush strokes you can create new brushes or edit existing brushes as described in detail in DrawPlus help.

Editing and copying brushes

At some point, you may want to edit either an existing preset brush or one you've created yourself. It's possible to edit and overwrite the existing brush preset but it is good practice to copy the brush to you own category at the same time as you perform brush editing. This prevents your presets from being modified from the originally installed presets. Both copying and editing are carried out by using the **Brush Edit** dialog.

Let's look at both edit and copy methods.

To edit a brush type:

1. Select a brush category from the Brushes tab.

2. Double-click on the preview icon of your chosen brush.

3. In the dialog, adjust the head, body or tail in the Brush Section Size. The head and tail can be isolated by either:

    - Setting the **Head (px)** and /or **Tail (px)** values in the Brush Section Size box.
    OR

    - Dragging the left or right blue vertical guides towards the centre of the preview window. Note how the Brush Section Size values change as you adjust each guide.

4. Choose to stretch or repeat the body of a brush by selection from the Body repeat method drop-down menu.

5. Optionally, your can swap the brush texture for another and modify the **Brush Name**. This will rename the existing brush.

6. Click the **OK** button.

This Edit method can only overwrite the existing brush properties. It does not allow you to save the brush type to a new category.

To copy a brush type:

- As for editing a brush type, but instead of double clicking right-click on the brush preview icon and select **Copy...**. This allows you to save the brush to a new brush name and to the current or a different brush category.

To delete a brush:

- Select a brush thumbnail, right-click and choose **Delete** from the submenu.

To edit the brush head and tail:

1. Select a brush type from the Brushes tab.

2. Right-click and choose **Edit...**. The dialog shows the brush texture in the preview window.

3. The head and tail can be isolated by either:

- Setting the **Head (px)** and /or **Tail (px)** values in the **Brush Section Size** box on the Brush Edit dialog.
  OR

- Dragging the left-most or right-most blue vertical guides towards the centre of the preview window. Note how the above values change as you adjust each guide.

4. Click the **OK** button.

Setting brush properties

All brushes, irrespective of whether they are vector, Bitmap, repeating or stretching, all have common properties, including brush type, colour, width, opacity, and smoothness. Using the Brushes context toolbar, you can adjust the properties of a drawn brush stroke once applied to your page.

Brush types applied to your brush strokes are handily listed in the **Document** folder of the Brushes tab. This useful snapshot is dynamic as it automatically updates if some brush types are no longer used, e.g. if its brush stroke has been deleted.

To change the brush properties of a brush stroke:

1. Select a previously drawn brush stroke—this displays the context toolbar above the workspace.

2. Change the brush design by double-clicking the **Brush** option, i.e.

The resulting Brush Edit dialog lets you swap the brush texture, modify the Brush Section Sizes (Head, Tail and Body) and modify the body repeating method for the brush stroke.
OR
Pick a Brush type from any category in the Brushes tab.

This will update all previously applied brush strokes using that brush type. The Brush presets in the Brushes tab will not be affected.

3. Use the **Colour..** button to change the brush stroke colour via a Colour Selector dialog.
OR
Pick a colour from the Colour tab or Swatches tab.

> Brush strokes cannot take a Gradient or Bitmap fill. If applied, the base colour of that fill will be adopted.

4. Alter the brush stroke **Width:** by setting a different point size using the slider (right arrow) or up/down arrows.
OR
Pick a line width from the Line tab.

5. The overall **Opacity** of the brush stroke can be adjusted using the slider (right arrow) or up/down arrows (100% opacity represents 0% Transparency; 0% Opacity means 100% Transparency (fully transparent)).
OR
Pick a transparency preset from the Transparency tab.

When the **Paintbrush Tool** is selected rather than a brush stroke, three additional options called **Smoothness**, **Select on Create**, and **Fill-on-Create** are shown on the context toolbar.

- To set the degree of smoothing to be applied to the brush stroke, set the **Smoothness** value (by entering a value or adjusting the slider).

- Enable ☐ Select-on-Create to leave the brush stroke selected on the page or, if disabled, leaves it deselected.

- Enable ◈ Fill-on-Create to fill the unclosed curve produced with a brush stroke with the default fill colour.

To change brush types:

1. Select the brush stroke.

2. Go to the Brushes tab and select firstly a brush category then a brush type from the displayed gallery. The brush stroke adopts the newly chosen brush.

Pressure sensitivity

Along with a brush's natural characteristics (its bristles, shape, and size), pressure sensitivity also plays a major part in how a brush is applied to your page. The extent to which a brush is applied is at the heart of an artist's creative ability. A heavily applied brush could help to convey strong imagery (e.g., moods), whereas a brush applied more lightly may indicate a more subtle effect.

In DrawPlus's world we apply pressure by using a pressure-sensitive device (a tablet and pen) and control how that pressure affects your brush stroke in DrawPlus's Pressure tab. This tab is used to apply different pressure profile presets, create your own profiles from scratch and adjusts how the brush's width and transparency changes as it responds to pressure. The maximum and minimum pressure can also be controlled via the tab—your brush strokes can appear more subtle or striking as a result.

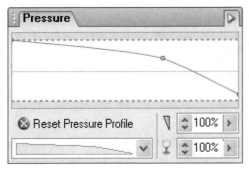

The pressure chart may appear a little daunting at first! It becomes a lot clearer if you imagine the chart when it is superimposed over the brush itself —it represents one half of a brush stroke along its entire length exactly. Of course, the same profile shape will be mirrored on the lower half of the stroke.

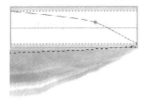

To apply a pressure profile:

1. Expand the Pressure tab at the bottom of your screen, and choose a pressure profile from the drop-down menu.

The pressure chart updates to reflect the chosen profile.

2. Apply a brush stroke to the page. This will adopt the chosen pressure profile.

The profile is maintained until you reset it or pick another profile from the preset list.

To create a new pressure profile:

1. Click the **Reset Pressure Profile** button. This sets the pressure chart back to default.

2. A turquoise line runs along the maximum pressure line at the top of the chart. Click on this line (the cursor changes) and drag downwards, moving the displayed red node into your chosen position. You now have a blue curve which represents the pressure profile.

3. Repeat the process for the number of nodes that you want to add to make up the profile.

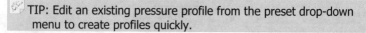

TIP: Edit an existing pressure profile from the preset drop-down menu to create profiles quickly.

You can then save the current pressure settings to your own saved pressure profile—this allows you to store and reapply your settings at any point in the future.

To save a new pressure profile:

1. In the Pressure tab, change the profile as described above.

2. Click on the ▷ **Tab Menu** button and select **Add Pressure Profile**.

Your new profile is automatically added to the bottom of the pressure profile preset drop-down list.

To delete a pressure profile:

1. Click on the ▷ **Tab Menu** button and select **Manage Pressure Profiles...**.

2. In the dialog, select the pressure profile for deletion and click the **Delete** button.

Altering brush width and opacity with pressure

For subtle brush pressure control, DrawPlus can vary the extent to which pen pressure can alter a brush's original width and opacity. This is expressed as a percentage of the original brush **Width** and **Opacity** values shown in the Brushes context toolbar. Imagine the end of your brush stroke tapering off or getting fainter as it lifts off the page—the concept is simple!

You can set the degree to which width and opacity changes either independently or in combination. Let's look at some examples... based on a **Default** brush called "Circle". The example doesn't use a natural media texture so the concept is illustrated more clearly. We'll use a pressure profile available from the preset drop-down menu for all examples.

Here's how the degree of width/opacity changes the brush stroke appearance.

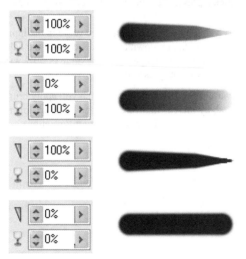

The first example shows the default behaviour when brush pressure is applied.

These settings are adjusted independently and are not stored with the pressure profiles.

To adjust brush width with pressure:

1. Select a previously drawn brush.

2. In the Pressure tab, pick a pressure profile from the drop-down menu.

3. Enter a **Width** value by setting a percentage value in the input box, using the slider or using the up/down arrows. The lower the value the less the pressure effects the brush width, i.e. a value of 50% will apply half the brush width under pressure.

To adjust opacity with pressure:

1. Select a previously drawn brush.

2. In the Pressure tab, pick a pressure profile from the drop-down menu.

3. Enter an **Opacity** value by setting a percentage value in the input box, using the slider or using the up/down arrows. The lower the value the less the pressure effects the brush opacity, i.e. a value of 50% will apply half the brush opacity under pressure.

You can set the pressure variance, i.e. the degree to which you apply brush pressure, via the Pressure tab by increasing/decreasing the lower or upper limits of the pressure chart. (See DrawPlus help for more information).

6
Text

Entering text

You can create different types of text in DrawPlus, i.e.

- **Artistic Text** - simply by typing directly onto the page (using the **Artistic Text Tool**) .

- **Frame Text** - by dragging a text frame and filling it with text (using the **Frame Text Tool**).

- **Shape Text** - by typing into a **QuickShape** or **drawn shape**.

In either case, it's easy to **edit the text** once it's created, by retyping it or altering properties like font, style, and point size.

In general, artistic text (as an independent object) is better suited to decorative or fancy typographic design, frame text is intended for presenting text passages in more traditional square or rectangular shaped blocks; shape text lends itself so well to blocks of body text where shape and flow contribute to the overall layout.

Artistic text behaves more independently than Shape and Frame Text and its individual letters can be stretched, rotated, sheared, enveloped, and combined with other objects. Shape text lacks a line property, but it conforms to the containing shape, and you can achieve unique text flow effects by varying the container's properties.

Maecenas condimentum tincidunt lorem. Vestibulum vel tellus. Sed vulputate. Morbi massa nunc, convallis a, commodo gravida, tincidunt sed, turpis. Aenean ornare viverra est. Maecenas lorem.

...Lorem ipsum.... dolor sit amet, consectetuer adipiscing elit. "Suspendisse erat massa, dapibus at."

Artistic Text   **Frame Text**   **Shape Text**

To enter new artistic text:

1. Select the [A] **Artistic Text Tool** on the Drawing toolbar's Text Tool flyout.

2. To create **artistic text** at the current default point size, click where you want to start the text.
   OR
   For artistic text that will be automatically sized into an area, click and drag out the area to the desired size.

3. To set text attributes (font, size, etc.) before you start typing, make selections on the Text context toolbar. To set colour prior to typing, set the Line/Fill swatches accordingly on the Studio's Colour or Swatches tab (see **Setting line properties** on p. 150 and **Setting fill properties** on p. 145).

4. Start typing.

To create frame text:

1. Select the [▤] **Framed Text Tool** on the Drawing toolbar's Text Tool flyout.

2. From the positioned cursor, either:

   - Double-click on the page or pasteboard to create a new frame at a default size.
     OR

   - Drag out a frame to your desired frame dimension.

3. (Optional) Set text and colour attributes before you start typing as described for artistic text.

4. Start typing within the frame.

Text frames will be drawn with a solid border by default. However, you can hide the border via **Layout>Display Text Frames** in **Tools>Options...** at any time.

To enter new shape text:

1. Create a shape either from the QuickShape flyout or by closing a drawn line.

2. With a shape still selected, just start typing. Text flows within the shape and the Artistic Text Tool is automatically selected.
OR
Select the Artistic Text Tool, then click in the centre of a shape (for a selection point inside the shape), set attributes on the Text context toolbar and Colour/Swatches tab if you wish, and start typing.

If you click on a text object with the Artistic Text Tool, you get an edit cursor in the text.

To extract text from a shape as an artistic text object:

- Right-click the shape and choose **Detach as New Object>Text**. You will then be able to move your text away from the object.

Except when you pre-drag to create artistic text, new text automatically appears at the default point size. It always takes **default settings** for font, style, line colour, fill, line weight, letter spacing, line spacing (leading), justification, etc. Default settings are stored separately for artistic text and shape text. Defaults for shape text are defined along with other shape defaults.

For more details about managing defaults, see **Updating Defaults** on p. 43.

With any type of text, if you press the **Enter** key while typing, you can type multiple lines of text as a single object.

Vivamus vel sapien. Praesent nisl tortor, laoreet eu, dapibus..

If you intend to use a large amount of text in your design you can adopt **Bullets and Numbering** to make lists or adjust default **Tab** positions, especially useful with Frame Text (see p. 95).

If you've typed more text into a shape than it can display, an 🄰 overflow symbol appears below the shape when it's selected. To attempt to reveal all the text, you can either enlarge the shape or reduce the size of the text (see **Fitting text to frames and shapes** on p. 101).

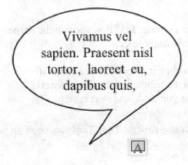

Once you have finished entering either type of text you can switch to one of the three selection tools and the object will be selected with handles. Then you can modify it just like any other graphics object. You can scale, rotate, skew, move, and copy it, and apply fills, line styles, and transparency, as well as a wide variety of **Special Effects** (see p. 219).

Working with Unicode text

On occasion, you may wish to import text in a foreign language, e.g. you may want to include a foreign quote in its original language. To work outside the standard ASCII character set, DrawPlus allows Unicode characters to be pasted (using **Edit>Paste...**) from the clipboard into your drawing.

To retain formatting, use "*Formatted Text (RTF)*" or for plain text use "*Unformatted Unicode Text*". For the latter, if your imported text appears as blocks instead, remember to apply a Unicode font such as Arial Unicode MS to fix the formatting.

Editing text

Once you've entered either **artistic**, **frame** or **shape text** (see **Entering Text** on p. 95), you can retype it and/or **format** its character attributes (font, style, point size, etc.), paragraph properties, and text flow. Text objects have **graphic properties**, too: artistic text behaves like an independent graphic object, while shape or frame text conforms to its container or frame.

You can add some design flair to your plain text, by using a very simple, but often overlooked, technique of varying the character point size or colour within a line of text. You can do this on-screen or via the **Edit Text window** by selecting just the characters you want to change... in the example below, the exclamation point is emphasised.

Selecting text

You can select any kind of text right on the page using the Artistic Text Tool, and then retype or reformat it. The displayed Text context toolbar provides convenient access to several basic attributes. The point size drop-down list shows the vertical size of the selected text in points. (The point is a traditional measure of the size of text; there are 72 points to the inch.)

The Text context toolbar displays a WYSIWYG listing of available fonts, and you can apply any font simply by selecting from the list when a text object has been previously selected! You'll get an alphabetic listing of font names, a sample of their appearance (as the font name and your page's selected text) and the font type (e.g., TrueType).

Retyping text

You can either retype artistic, frame or shape text directly on the page via the Artistic Text Tool, or use the Edit Text window—great for managing large amounts of text (overflowed shape text or otherwise) in a simple word processing environment.

To retype text on the page:

1. Select the object and the **A** **Artistic Text Tool** (from the Drawing toolbar's Text flyout), in either order.

2. Type new text at the selection point or drag to select text, cut then retype. To cut, copy, and paste, use the toolbar buttons or standard Windows keyboard shortcuts.

To retype text in the Edit Text window:

1. Right-click on the text object and choose **Text>Edit Text...**. The **Edit Text** window appears with the text ready for editing.

2. Type new text at the selection point or drag to select text, cut then retype. To cut, copy, and paste, use the toolbar buttons or standard Windows keyboard shortcuts. To start a new line, press the **Enter** key.

3. To return to DrawPlus, click the 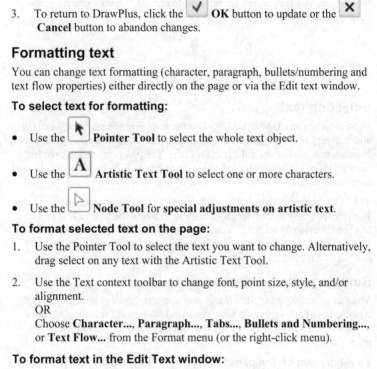 **OK** button to update or the **✗** **Cancel** button to abandon changes.

Formatting text

You can change text formatting (character, paragraph, bullets/numbering and text flow properties) either directly on the page or via the Edit text window.

To select text for formatting:

*   Use the **Pointer Tool** to select the whole text object.

*   Use the **Artistic Text Tool** to select one or more characters.

*   Use the **Node Tool** for **special adjustments on artistic text**.

To format selected text on the page:

1. Use the Pointer Tool to select the text you want to change. Alternatively, drag select on any text with the Artistic Text Tool.

2. Use the Text context toolbar to change font, point size, style, and/or alignment.
    OR
    Choose **Character...**, **Paragraph...**, **Tabs...**, **Bullets and Numbering...**, or **Text Flow...** from the Format menu (or the right-click menu).

To format text in the Edit Text window:

1. Right-click on the text object and choose **Text>Edit Text...**.

2. Apply different attributes: font, point size, bold, and italic. Select the letters or words you want to change with the cursor, and then use the buttons on the toolbar to apply properties to it.

3. To return to DrawPlus, click the **✓** **OK** button to update, or the **✗** **Cancel** button to abandon changes.

Click **A͟4 Show Formatting** to switch between unformatted (draft) and formatted view—use the unformatted view for editing lots of text at once.

For special adjustments on artistic text:

- Select the object and the **Node Tool**, in either order. Adjustment sliders and handles appear (as if you'd selected a **QuickShape**) to the left, top and bottom of the text (this won't work for shape text). Move the mouse pointer over a slider to see its function.

  - Adjust the Wrap slider inward to change line wraps onto a new line).

  - Adjust the Leading slider to change leading (space between lines).

  - Adjust the Letter slider to change tracking (space between characters).

- To move a single character, select and drag the square handle at its bottom-left corner.

- To rotate a single character (opposite), click its handle and drag the node on the opposite end of the displayed line to either side.

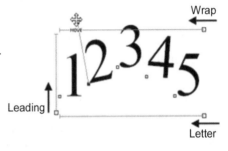

- TIP: Use the **Shift** key after selecting a letter to constrain movement horizontally or vertically. If you want to move a group of letters, select them one at a time with the **Shift** key held down.

Fitting text to frames and shapes

Resizing

- You can resize frame or shape text (change its point size) automatically when resizing frame and shapes. First make sure the **Scale text with object** box is checked in the Text flow dialog (right-click **Text>Text Flow...**) then drag a corner of the selected text object. Using an a example shape, here's how the original shape (on the left) appears after being enlarged with (centre) and without (right) the setting being checked:

Positioning

- **Vertical alignment** (right-click **Text>Text Flow...**) moves existing text to the Top, Bottom, or Centre of the container (alternatively you can justify text vertically). The setting anchors a particular part of the object—for example, a "Top" setting anchors the top line and forces new text to come in below, while a "Bottom" setting anchors the bottom (most recent) line and pushes previous lines up as you type new lines.

- To add white space around your text, you can indent text from the frame or shape edge via right-click **Text>Text Flow....** Values can be set to indent from Left, Right, Top and/or Bottom.

Text overflow

If there's too much text to fit into a text frame or shape, the  **Overflow** button appears beneath the shape; DrawPlus stores the overflowing text in an invisible overflow area. To reduce the text content you might edit the story down to allow text to fit in a frame sequence. However, fitting the text precisely into the frame or shape may be preferable (it's also a great time saver!).

- Click the **Overflow** button to attempt an **AutoFit** of frame or shape text.
  OR

- Use the **Autofit**, **Enlarge Text** or **Shrink Text** on the text context toolbar.

Adding dimension lines and labels

DrawPlus lets you add **dimension lines** with text **labels** showing the distance between two fixed points in a drawing, or the angle formed by three points. For example, you can draw a dimension line along one side of a box, measuring the distance between the two corner points. If you resize the box, the line automatically follows suit, and its label text updates to reflect the new measurement.

The 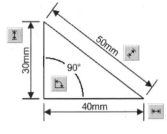 **Dimension Tool** is available from the Line flyout on the Drawing toolbar. When selected, its Dimensions context toolbar displays four tool options, their buttons shown in the illustration along with the kind of dimension line each one draws:

 Vertical

Horizontal

Slanted

Angular

(Slanted dimension lines can be drawn at any angle.)

To draw a dimension:

1. Select the **Dimension Tool** from the Drawing toolbar's Line flyout. (The flyout shows the icon of the most recently selected tool.) Choose the appropriate tool option from the Dimension context toolbar.

   Although they can be drawn anywhere on the page, dimension lines are at their most accurate when attached to **connection points** on objects (see p. 66). When you choose one of the Dimension tools, connection points on page objects become visible on hover over, i.e. when you move the mouse pointer directly over a connection point, a small box appears around it when a connection can be made. For more information on connection points, see Connectors on p. 66.

2. For a **linear dimension** (vertical, horizontal, or slanted), click where you want to start the dimension line (e.g., on a connection point), then drag and release the mouse button where you want to end the line (maybe on another connection point). The illustration below shows the result of dragging between connection points A and B. A pair of parallel **extension lines** appears from the two points. Between the two extension lines, the dimension line and its label "float," awaiting final positioning.

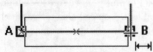

To complete the dimension line, move the mouse again to position the floating line and its label—note that they respond independently—and click when they are where you want them. (You can always change the positions later.) The dimension line appears.

OR

For an **angular dimension**, click a point along one side of the desired angle, then drag and release the mouse button at a point along the other side of the angle (points A and B in the illustration below). Click again at the vertex of the angle (point C below). These three points define the starting and ending sides of the angle. Between the two sides, the angle's arc and its label "float," awaiting final positioning. Click again to position the floating elements

Angles are measured counter-clockwise from the starting to the ending side, so choose your three nodes accordingly.

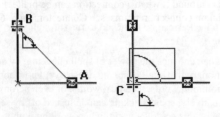

3. To complete the dimension line, move the mouse again to position the floating line or arc and its label—note that they respond independently—and click when they are where you want them. (You can always change the positions later.) The dimension line appears.

Once you've added a dimension line, you can use the [⊳] **Node Tool** to freely adjust node and label positions. Use **Format>Character** to change the font, font size, colour and style of the label text. You can also format the line, including line colour, width, style, or adjust the level of precision with the context toolbar.

Spell-checking

The **Spell Checker** lets you check the spelling of selected artistic text or shape text or all text sequentially throughout your DrawPlus document.

Multilingual spell checking is supported by use of over 10 spelling dictionaries. By default, the spelling dictionary is set on program install (according to Windows Control Panel's Regional and Language Options), i.e. your dictionary is set to the operating system's language. However, if you want to spell check against a different language this can be selected from **Tools>Options>Spell Checker** at any time.

between the pair. The clock struck midnight.. the man was gone, forver into the mist-clad night.

Whichever language is used, any detected spelling mistakes or any word not present in the language's dictionary will appear underlined with a red zigzag line if the **Underline mistakes as you type** option is used. This is great for visually checking text in its original context (e.g., the word "forever" is misspelt as "forver" opposite).

Alternatively, the **Spell Checker** can be launched to run through your document, spell checking as it goes.

With either method, you can enhance the power of spell checking, by adding words to the current dictionary that spell checking doesn't yet know about. These could include uncommon words, technical words, or even acronyms and abbreviations. Alternatively, spell checking can be turned off by selecting "None" as a language type—this could be useful when working with text containing an unmanageable number of unusual terms (perhaps scientific or proprietary terminology).

To check spelling:

1. (Optional) To check specific text, select the artistic, frame or shape text in advance.

2. Choose **Check Spelling...** from the Tools menu.

3. (Optional) In the dialog, click **Options...** to set preferences for ignoring words in certain categories, such as words containing numbers or domain names.

4. Enable **Check currently selected objects only** or **Check all text in the drawing** radio buttons depending on if you want to spell check text selected previously or all text.

5. Click **Start** to begin the spelling check.

When a problem is found, DrawPlus highlights the problem word on the page. The dialog offers alternative suggestions, and you can choose to **Change** or **Ignore** this instance (or all instances with **Change All** or **Ignore All**) of the problem word, with the option of using **Add** to add the problem word to your dictionary. DrawPlus will also let you **Suggest** an alternative.

6. Spell checking continues until you click the **Close** button or the spell-check is completed.

To change to a different spelling language:

1. Go to **Options...** from the Tools menu, and select **Spell Checker**.

2. Choose a different Language from the drop-down menu, and click **OK**.

To check the spelling of a single word:

1. With **Underline mistakes as you type** checked (in **Tools>Options>Spell Checker**), select in a marked word, then right-click. You'll see alternative spellings on the context menu.

2. To replace the word, choose an alternative spelling from the menu.

3. To tell DrawPlus to ignore (leave unmarked) all instances of the marked word in the publication, choose **Ignore All**.

4. To add the marked word (as spelled) to your personal dictionary, choose **Add to Dictionary**. This means DrawPlus will ignore the word in any drawing.

You can also run the Spell Checker from the context menu by choosing **Check Spelling...**.

Font substitutions

DrawPlus will allow font substitution after opening PDF files or third-party DrawPlus documents; this is necessary when original fonts used in the documents are not available on your own PC. If this occurs, font substitution can be performed when the .PDF or .DPP file is opened.

When opening a file, font substitution can be initiated from the message:

"The following fonts used by "<file name>" are no longer available.
<FONT LIST>
Would you like to edit the font substitutions".

From this point, two options are open to you:

- Click **Yes**, to access DrawPlus's **Substitute Missing Fonts** dialog, i.e. to allow you to swap detected missing fonts with fonts of your choosing.

- Click **No**, to automatically swap missing fonts without prompting.

> If a font is unavailable and has been substituted, its font name on the Text context toolbar is prefixed by the "?" character.

The dialog allows missing fonts to be replaced by available fonts selected from a font list. The available fonts are those currently installed on your PC. It's also possible to add more than one font to act as a replacement, which is particularly useful if you want to provide an alternative to your first choice substituted font, e.g. a more widely available font such as Verdana, Arial or Times New Roman could act as a secondary font.

Clearly, the process of substituting large numbers of fonts is time-consuming, repetitive and most importantly document specific only. As a solution, especially if the same substitutions need to be applied between different DrawPlus documents in the future, you can export all your font mappings to a single Serif Font Map (*.SFM) file which can subsequently be imported into other documents—saving you the effort of recreating the mappings again (use the dialog's **Import** and **Export** buttons). The SFM file replaces the font mapping information stored within the publication.

To substitute a font:

1. Select **Font Substitutions...** from the Tools menu.

2. In the **Substitute Missing Fonts** dialog, select a missing font from the **Font to substitute** drop-down menu.

3. Choose a replacement font from the Available fonts list box ensuring that the **Bold** and/or **Italic** options are checked if necessary. Some fonts may be a more acceptable substitute with the bold or italic style set.

4. Click **Add<<** to place the font in the **Substitute with** box. This box can contain more than one font—your first choice and a secondary font (e.g. Arial or Times New Roman). You should always place your first choice at the top of the list with the **Move up** or **Move down** buttons.

5. Go back to Step 3 and substitute each missing font in the **Font to substitute** drop-down menu in turn.

For PDF imports especially, if you want all new documents to utilize the font substitutions used in your current document, use **Tools>Save Settings to** make the current font substitutions your default.

7

Working with Objects

Copying, pasting, cutting, and deleting objects

To copy one or more objects to the Windows Clipboard: :

1. Select the object(s).

2. Click the 🗗 **Copy** button on the Standard toolbar.

If you're using another Windows application, you can usually copy and paste objects via the Clipboard.

To paste an object from the Clipboard:

*   Click the 🗗 **Paste** button on the Standard toolbar.

The standard Paste command inserts a clipboard object onto the page.

> To select the type of object to be pasted from the Clipboard, choose **Paste Special...** from the Edit menu.

To cut one or more objects to the Clipboard:

1. Select the object(s).

2. Click the ✂ **Cut** button on the Standard toolbar.

The object is deleted from the page and a copy is placed on the Windows Clipboard.

To delete one or more objects:

*   Select the object(s) with the Pointer, Rotate or Node Tool and press the **Delete** key.
    OR

*   View the Layers tab, expand your chosen layer, select an object entry that is present on that layer, then press the **Delete** key. Use **Ctrl**-click to select multiple objects for deletion.

Cloning an object

Besides using the Windows Clipboard to cut, copy and paste objects, you can "clone" or duplicate objects easily using drag-and-drop, and duplicate multiple copies of any object. For duplication, a copy is displayed at the new location and the original object is still kept at the same position—your new copy also possesses the formatting of the original copied object.

To:	**Do this:**
Create an exact copy (duplicate)	Select the object while holding down the **Ctrl** key, then drag the copied object to a new position.
	To constrain the position of the copy (to same horizontal or vertical), press and hold down the **Shift** key simultaneously while dragging. A duplicate of the object appears at the new location.
Make a grid of multiple copies	Select the object, then choose **Replicate...** from the Tools menu.
Make copies that are slightly different from each other	Select the object, then choose **Transform...** from the Tools menu.
Make a copy that is larger or smaller	Select the object, then choose **Create Contour...** from the Tools menu.
Apply the object's formatting to another object (line and fill)	Use the **Format Painter** button from the Standard toolbar.

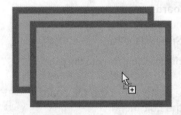

 TIP: Use duplication when rotating or shearing an object—the result is a new copy at a new angle, possibly overlapping the original object.

Making multiple copies

If you need to clone single or multiple objects, you can use the **Replicate** feature to avoid repetitive copy and paste operations. For example, you can specify three columns and four rows, for twelve identical copies. The single dialog also has the option of letting DrawPlus determine the X and Y spacing (horizontal and vertical gap) between objects. The feature comes in handy for creating repetitive patterns or producing artwork for label sheets

To replicate an object:

1. Select an object. Remember to size the object to be cloned and place it in a convenient starting position—usually the top-left of the page.

2. Choose **Replicate...** from the Tools menu.

3. In the dialog, set the Grid size by choosing number of columns or rows. Objects are cloned into this grid arrangement (but can be moved subsequently into any position).

4. Set an X and Y spacing (horizontal and vertical gap) between objects if necessary.

5. Click **OK**.

For multiple objects on different layers, you can right-click on a layer and check the item **Edit All Layers**. Now, instead of working with the layers one at a time, we can include all objects (once selected) on all layers, permitting perfect replication.

Applying a transform

The Transform feature lets you make multiple copies of one or more selected objects, with a transformation applied to each successive copy in the series. Transforms are a great way to generate elements for a Stopframe animation sequence involving rotation or directional changes (see p. 174).

To create a transform:

1. Select an object then choose **Transform...** from the Tools menu.

2. From the dialog, specify the type of transformation (rotation and/or scaling), the number of copies, and a positional offset between copies.

For example, you can transform a circle into an interesting shell shape by choosing 2° rotation, 93% scaling, 50 copies, and an X offset of 0.5cm.

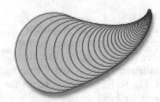

You can reposition one or more selected objects by using the Transform tab.

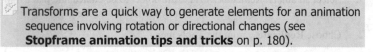

Transforms are a quick way to generate elements for an animation sequence involving rotation or directional changes (see **Stopframe animation tips and tricks** on p. 180).

Making a larger or smaller copy for contouring

The **Create Contour** function lets you reproduce a single object slightly larger or smaller than the original, for border or perspective effects. For example, you can create outlines around text or create a second object to **blend** with the first (see opposite).

To apply contours:

1. Select the object you want to reproduce.

2. Choose **Create Contour...** from the Tools menu.

3. Use the dialog to specify the degree of difference (Small, Medium, Large or Custom) and position of the new object with respect to the original (i.e., Outside or Inside).

4. Click **OK**. A reduced copy appears in front of the original object; an enlarged copy appears behind it. The new object always has a black line and white fill, but it's selected so you can apply a custom line and fill right away.

Making "in-between" copies of two objects

Blending is yet another useful way of making multiple copies by in-betweening two different objects for a "morphing" effect. Impressive 3D effects can be achieved. For details, see **Creating blends** on p. 224.

Copying an object's formatting

Format Painter is used to copy one object's line and fill properties directly to another object, including between line/shape and text objects.

To apply one object's formatting to another:

1. Select the object whose formatting you wish to copy.

2. Click the ⬜ **Format Painter** button on the Standard toolbar. When you click the button, the selected object's formatting is "picked up."

3. Click another object to apply the first object's formatting to it. The second object becomes selected.

4. To select another object without pasting the formatting, click it with the **Shift** key down.

5. To cancel Format Painter mode, press **Esc**, click on a blank area, or choose any tool button.

For copy formatting from one text object to another, a number of other text properties (font, style, and so on) besides line and fill are passed along at the same time.

Moving objects

You can move any selected object anywhere you want and drop it back onto the page or pasteboard by releasing the mouse button.

To move one or more objects:

1. Select the object(s) with one of the selection tools (Pointer, Rotate, or Node).

2. ⬚ Click within the selection (not on a handle) and drag to a new location by holding down the left mouse button. Note that the Pointer cursor changed to become a Move cursor.

3. Release the mouse button at the new location.

To nudge an object in increments:

- Select the object(s) and use the keyboard arrows (up, down, left, right). These move the selection by the currently set **Nudge Distance** per key press—set the value in the Layout pane in **Tools>Options...**.

For even finer control, hold down the **Ctrl** key while pressing keyboard arrows to nudge the selection only 1/10 as far with each key press.

To constrain the movement to horizontal or vertical:

- Press and hold down the **Shift** key <u>after</u> you begin dragging the selection, then release the **Shift** key <u>after</u> you release the left mouse button.

For precise movements, you can enter exact 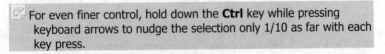 **Horizontal Position** or **Vertical Position** values in the Transform tab; then set an anchor point to dictate from which part of the object the movement is to take place—from a corner, edge midpoint, or centre.

Splitting objects

It is possible to split any single object or group of vector objects (or bitmaps for that matter) by using the **Knife Tool**. You can cut along a freeform line drawn across your object(s), leaving you with separate "child" objects as fragments of the original.

Simple or more impressive special effects can be achieved either by a single knife cut across the object or by sweeping the knife cut in and out of the object multiple times in a zig-zag pattern.

To split objects:

1. Select one or more objects.

   TIP: Ensure **Edit All Layers** button on Layers tab is enabled if you want to cut through selected objects on multiple layers.

2. Select the ![knife icon] **Knife Tool** on the Drawing Toolbar's Vector Edit flyout.

3. (Optional) Use **Smoothness** on the tool's context toolbar to set how regular the freeform cutting line is—click the right arrow and drag the slider right for increasing smoothness.

4. Using the cursor, drag a freeform line across any object(s) you would like to split (unselected objects on which the line traverses will not be split).

5. (Optional) With the Pointer tool, you can drag the newly split objects apart as required.

Erasing and adding to objects

DrawPlus lets you take a "virtual" eraser to your drawing, letting you remove portions of your selected object(s) on an individual layer or across multiple layers. The extent of erasing can be controlled depending on the tool's currently set erasing width and pressure setting (if using a graphics tablet).

The flipside of erasing is "adding to" (i.e., augmenting), a technique to add or "grow" a vector objects' boundaries—great for reshaping an existing object or to grow a vector shape from scratch. This may be especially useful when creating an unusual filled shape.

Erasing   **Adding to**

To erase portions of a selected object:

1. Select the 🖉 **Erase Tool** on the Drawing Toolbar's Vector Edit flyout.

2. (Optional) From the context toolbar, choose a **Nib** style (circle, square, or diamond) and/or set a **Width** to define the erase width that will be cut.

3. Position the 🖑 cursor, and drag over an object's edge. You'll see the area to be erased area being drawn temporarily (use the **Ctrl** key to redefine the erase area while drawing).

4. Release the mouse button to erase the area drawn.

To add to a selected object:

1. Select the 🖌 **Freeform Paint Tool** on the Drawing Toolbar's Vector Edit flyout.

2. (Optional) From the context toolbar, set a **Width** to defines the nib width which will be drawn.

3. (Optional) Disable **Select-on-Create** if you want to create new objects every time you use the tool (you might want to create a series of shapes without switching tools).

4. Position the 🖑 cursor over the object and drag over an object boundary. You'll see blue shading which represents the area to be added. (You can use the **Ctrl** key to redefine the painted area while holding down the mouse button).

5. Release the mouse button to reshape the object to include the newly drawn area.

If you add to or erase from a bitmap, QuickShape, or artistic text, they will be converted to curves, preventing further editing in their original form.

For **Stopframe animation**, consider using either tool as a quick way to modify object shapes frame-by-frame.

Resizing objects

To resize an object (in general):

1. Select the object(s) with the **Pointer Tool**.

2. Position the cursor over one of the object's handles—you will notice that the cursor changes to a double-headed Size cursor. Click one of the selection's handles and drag it to a new position.

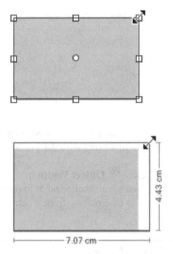

Dragging from an edge handle resizes in one dimension, by moving that edge. Dragging from a corner handle (above) resizes in two dimensions, by moving two edges, while maintaining the selection's aspect ratio (proportions).

Note that when resizing any altered object dimensions will be temporarily displayed during the operation (this **Tool Feedback** can be switch on/off in **Tools>Options>Ease of Use**).

To allow free resizing of an object to any aspect ratio:

- With the **Shift** key depressed, drag from an object's corner handle.

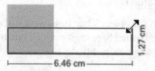

- If you drag an object's side handles, you'll stretch or squash the object in one direction.

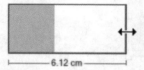

You can also resize objects using the keyboard arrows, via **Size Objects...** (Tools menu), and make fine resizing adjustments with the Transform tab.

For precise resizing, you can enter exact ^{W} **Object Width** or ^{H} **Object Height** values in the Transform tab; then set an anchor point to dictate from which part of the object the resizing is to take place—from a corner, edge midpoint, or centre.

Rotating and shearing objects

The **Rotate Tool** lets you both rotate and shear (slant) one or more objects. For a 3D shear effect, use the **Perspective flyout**.

To rotate one or more objects around a centre point:

1. Click the 🔄 **Rotate Tool** button on the Drawing toolbar's Selection Tool flyout.

2. Click to select the object(s), then hover over a corner handles and, when you see the cursor change, drag in the direction in which you want to rotate the object.

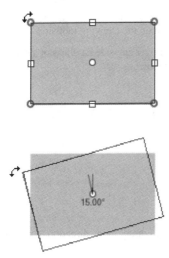

You'll notice the angle of rotation displayed around the object's centre of rotation ⊙.

3. Release the mouse (use **Shift** key for 15 degree intervals).

> You can also use the Rotate Tool to move and copy objects.

To change the centre point of rotation:

1. Move the centre of rotation ⊙ away from its original position to any position on the page. The marker can also be moved to be outside the object—ideal for rotating grouped objects around a central point.

2. Drag the rotate pointer to a new rotation angle—the object will rotate about the new pivot.

> Don't confuse the rotation centre marker with the anchor point available in the Transform tab. While you can use the latter for rotating objects about their corners, edges or the object centre, the Rotate Tool's centre marker sets a custom rotation point for more complex rotations.

Besides being able to rotate an object, the Rotate Tool allows you to skew or "shear" it.

To shear or copy shear an object:

1. Select the 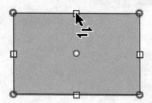 **Rotate Tool** button on the Drawing toolbar.

2. Click to select the object(s), hover over any side handle (not a corner handle) until you see the Shear cursor.

3. Hold the mouse down and drag the pointer in the direction in which you want to shear the object, then release.

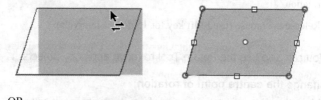

    OR

*   Select the object, go to the Transform tab and enter a ⬜ **Shear** value.

To copy shear, use the **Ctrl** key while dragging—this preserves the original object, while shearing the new copied object as you drag.

To undo the rotation or shear (restore the original object):

*   Double-click the object.

DrawPlus also provides the following methods for controlling rotation. (These don't apply to shear.)

To rotate an object 90° counter-clockwise:

- Select the object(s) with any selection tool and click the **Rotate 90°** button on the Standard toolbar.

To rotate an object by a numeric value:

1. Select the object(s) with any selection tool and choose **Rotate** from the Arrange menu.

2. Select a specific rotation value from the submenu, or select **Custom...** to display a dialog that lets you enter a precise numeric value.

For precise rotation and shear, you can enter an exact **Rotation** or **Shear** value in the Transform tab; then set an **Anchor point** to dictate which part of the object the rotation/shear is to take place—from a corner, edge midpoint or centre.

Flipping objects

You can flip objects horizontally (left to right; top and bottom stay the same) or vertically (top to bottom; left and right stay the same).

To flip an object:

- Select the object(s) with one of the selection tools (Pointer, Rotate, or Node).

- To flip the selection left to right, click the **Flip Horizontal** button on the Standard toolbar, or choose **Flip Horizontal** from the Arrange menu. (Top and bottom stay the same.)

- To flip the selection top to bottom, click the **Flip Vertical** button on the Standard toolbar, or choose **Flip Vertical** from the Arrange menu. (Left and right stay the same.)

Finding objects

When you create any object in your Drawplus drawing you're actually creating an object name for that drawing. This serves several purposes: to uniquely identify objects when using the Layers tab and to allow objects to be targeted by ActionScript (in Keyframe animation).

Object names are visible in the Layers tab—they are created on a selected layer automatically as you draw the object. Many objects are given the same names such as "Bitmap", "Quick Ellipse", "Curve, 2 Nodes"; you may like to rename each object to make them distinct from each other (making them clearly identifiable).

For more advanced drawings, the naming of each drawing component is not viable due to drawing complexities. This is because a large number of objects may make up an identifiable design (such as bird like the Robin below) and to name them would be time-consuming and serve little benefit (why name a single brush stroke?). Instead it makes sense to name the "collective" group rather than the individual objects that make up the group.

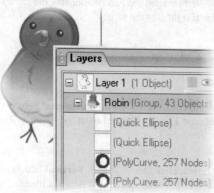

DrawPlus not only searches for individual named objects but named groups as well. This allows you to locate an object/group to allow resizing, rotating, transform, change colour, or any other operation. For either, you can use the Find Object dialog which locates the object or group on the current layer (shown), page or document.

Find Object

Find What:

Robin

Look In:

Current Layer

Partial matching (default) or whole word matching is possible in the search. Enable the **Match Whole Word** check box for the latter. If more than one object is located, then clicking the **Find Next** button will jump to the next object, selecting each one in turn.

 Objects or groups that have not been named manually will never be included in the search.

To change an object's or group's name:

1. In the Layers tab, expand the layer entry to which an object or group belongs.

2. Select the object/group, then click on its name.

3. At the insertion point, type a new name then either press **Enter** or click away from the tab.

To find an object or group:

1. Select **Find Object...** from the Edit menu.

2. From the dialog, enter the individual object or group name you want to search for in the **Find What** box. As partial matching is supported by default you can also search for the beginning of objects' names, i.e. searching for "frog" would locate objects named "frog1", "frog2", "frogs legs", etc.

3. In the **Look In** drop-down menu, restrict the search to the Current Layer or Current Page. Alternatively, search throughout the Whole Document.

4. (Optional) Limit your search to **Match Whole Word** or **Match Case** by enabling the check boxes. To search from the bottom of your layers upward, check the **Search Up** check box.

5. Click the **Find Next** button to perform your search. The first matching object is shown selected and zoomed to selection (ready for editing!).

6. (Optional) For more than one object located, click the **Find Next** button again to jump to the next matching object.

Locking/unlocking an Object

So you may have moved or resized a few objects and don't want to risk moving, resizing or deleting them. The solution is to lock them to prevent accidental changes from occurring.

To lock an object:

1. Select the single or grouped object.

2. Choose **Arrange>Lock Position**. When you try to select the object the cursor changes to a lock symbol.

> You can still alter a locked object's fill, line, or transparency properties.

To unlock an object:

1. Select the single or grouped object.

2. Use the **Arrange>Unlock Position** command. Now you'll see a normal cursor again.

Grouping objects

The advantage of converting a set of objects into a group is that it is easier to select and edit the objects all at the same time. The only requirement for grouping is that multiple objects are selected in advance (see p. 49).

To create a group from a multiple selection:

- Click the 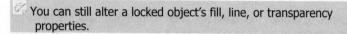 **Group selected items** button below the selection.
  OR

  Click the **Group/Ungroup** button on the Standard toolbar. (To change the group back into a multiple selection, pick the same button.)

To ungroup (turn a group back into a multiple selection):

- Click the **Ungroup selected group** button below the selection.
  OR
  Click the **Group/Ungroup** button again (Standard toolbar).

Once grouped, simply clicking on any member of a group selects the group object. In general, any operation you carry out on the group affects each member of the group. Property changes applied to a group—such as changing line or fill—will alter all the objects that make up the group.

Objects within groups can be selected and edited without having to ungroup your grouped objects—text can be edited, the node tool applied, line and fill properties can be changed. In fact you can edit any grouped object as you would its ungrouped counterpart. This avoids the headache of having to reassemble the group after editing an individual object!

To select an individual object within a group:

- **Ctrl**-click on the object. The object is selected as for any ungrouped object.

You can then edit the object, then click away to deselect the group.

Combining, cropping, and joining objects

DrawPlus includes some powerful tools to carve new shapes out of old shapes—the **Combine**, **Crop**, **Clip**, **Add**, **Subtract**, and **Intersect** buttons on the Standard toolbar! Combine, Crop and Clip work a bit differently from Add, Subtract and Intersect (considered as "Join" commands). It's worth keeping the distinctions in mind:

- With Combine, Crop and Clip, you're creating a temporary composite object where two or more component objects used to overlap. This combination, like a group, can be broken apart later with **Crop>Uncrop** on the Arrange menu.

- With the Join commands, you actually produce a permanent new object out of any selected objects. The action can't be reversed, except by using the **Undo** command. A Joined object can be edited with the Node Tool, while a combined, cropped or clipped object cannot.

 Combine

Merges two or more objects into a composite object, with a clear "hole" where their filled regions overlap. The composite takes the line and fill of the bottom object. Click button again to **Break Apart**.

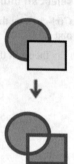

Crop and
Clip flyout

Provides four cropping or
clipping functions as
follows:

• Crop to Top

The bottom object is
cropped to the outline of
the top object.

• Crop to Bottom

The top object is cropped
to the outline of the
bottom object.

• Clip to Top

The bottom object is
clipped to the outline of
the top object.

• Clip to Bottom   The top object is clipped
                    to the outline of the
                    bottom object.

 Join/Add   Creates one new object
                    that's the sum of any two
                    selected objects, whether
                    or not they overlap.

 Join/Subtract   Discards the overlap
                    between the top and
                    bottom object. The top
                    object is also discarded.

                    Useful as a quick way of
                    truncating shapes and
                    pictures with another
                    object.

 Join/Intersect like Subtract, requires overlapping objects—it retains the overlap and discards the rest.

Aligning and distributing objects

Alignment involves taking a group of selected objects and aligning them all in one operation—the operation is applied to all of the objects selected. The alignment's behaviour is different depending on how multiple objects are selected, i.e.

- by **Shift-click**: If you select each object in turn by **Shift**-click, the alignment of selected objects is always performed relative to the edges of the **last** selected object (unless alignment relative to the page is set).

- by **Marquee**: If you drag a marquee over the objects (or use **Edit>Select All**), the objects always align relative to the edges of the object which is farthest back in the z-order (unless alignment relative to the page is set).

For example, top alignment will align objects to the top edge of a square (shown below) if it was selected last or if all objects were selected by marquee (assumes the square is the farthest back object). Bottom alignment would align to the bottom edge of a square.

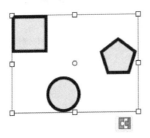 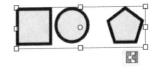

Alignment controls are available in the Align tab or from **Arrange>Align Objects**. Both sets of controls let you distribute objects, so that your objects (as a multiple selection) are spread evenly between the endmost objects on your page. Alternatively, check the **Spaced** option and corresponding measurement value to set a specific distance between each object.

To align two or more objects:

1. Using the Pointer Tool, **Shift**-click on all the objects you want to align, or draw a marquee box around them (or use **Edit>Select All**), to create a multiple selection.

2. In the Align tab, select an option for vertical alignment (Top, Vertical Centre, or Bottom) or horizontal alignment (Left, Horizontal Centre, Right) of an object. Object is the last selected object for **Shift**-click multiple selection or the farthest back in Z-order for marquee multiple selection.

To align one or more objects with a page edge:

- Follow the steps above, but check the **Include Page** option.

If selected, the page is added to the set of objects included in the alignment, e.g. selecting **Align Top** aligns all of the objects in the selection to the top of the page. If only one object is selected, page-edge alignment is automatic.

To distribute two or more objects:

1. Using the Pointer Tool, **Shift**-click on all the objects you want to distribute, or draw a marquee box around them, to create a multiple selection.

2. In the Align tab, select the **Horizontal Distribute** or **Vertical Distribute** option to distribute objects vertically or horizontally, respectively.

3. Check the **Spaced** option to set a fixed distance between vertically or horizontally distributed objects (otherwise the objects distribute evenly between endmost items).

Ordering objects

If the concept of **ordering** is new to you, think of the objects on a page as being stacked or piled on top of each other. The front-most object is the one on top of the stack. Each time you create a new object, it goes in front of the objects already there. But you can move any object to any **level** in the ordering sequence, and obtain sophisticated drawing effects by learning how to manipulate the front/back relationship of objects.

There are four possibilities for ordering objects but not all of them are always available. If you have selected an object that is on top of all others you will have the options **Send to Back** and **Back One** - you can't bring it forward because it's on the top "level" of the stack. Conversely, for an object at the bottom of a stack you will have the options **Bring to Front** or **Forward One**. All the options are available for objects that are neither at the top or bottom.

As an example, here's a dissected view of the object order used to create a picture of a corkscrew.

All the component objects have been detached from the completed drawing.

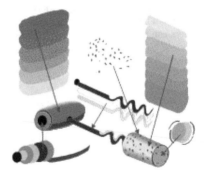

Notice how the artist achieved a "3D" look for the handle and cork by blending, resulting in "stacks" of progressively smaller shapes, using differently coloured fills graded from dark to light.

Effects like reflections, metallic highlights, shadows, and contours are just a few of the possibilities that you can explore using object ordering.

Don't confuse the concept of object ordering with that of layers in the document.

To change the object's position in the stacking order:

-  To shift the selected object's position behind other objects (on the bottom), choose the **Send to Back** button from the Standard toolbar.

- To shift the selected object's position to the front of other objects (on top), choose the **Bring to Front** button from the Standard toolbar.

- To shift the object's position one step toward the front, choose **Arrange>Order Objects>Forward One**.

- To shift the object's position one step toward the back, and choose **Arrange>Order Objects>Back One**.

Working with layers

If you are drawing something simple, you don't really need to make use of layers—you can do all your work on the single layer that every new document has. However, if you're creating something a little more tricky then layers can be a vital aid in separating objects into independent sets. You can think of layers as transparent sheets of paper upon which you can draw your objects.

Layers are useful when you're working on a complex design where it makes sense to separate one cluster of objects from another. The whole drawing is produced by piling up the layers and viewing all of the objects on all of the layers; you can choose which layer you are editing and thus make changes without fear of modifying anything on another layer. In essence, by building up your drawing from multiple layers you make it much easier to edit.

Each layer is situated along with other layers (if present) within a stack on the **Layers tab**—the uppermost layer is applied over any lower layer on the page. You can also expand each layer entry to view an object(s) associated with that layer (see the "Sky" layer opposite). Each object entry can be clicked to select the object in your workspace, and you can **name** your objects at any time.

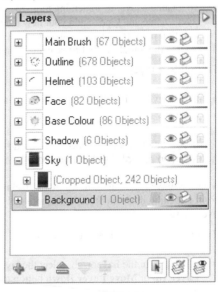

The tab allows layers to be created, renamed, deleted, reordered, frozen, and merged.

The thumbnail previews act as a useful to identify each layer—hover your cursor over for a larger preview.

In order to create a new object on a particular layer, you'll first need to "activate" (select) that layer.

To display the Layers tab:

- Go to **View>Studio Tabs** and check **Layers Tab**, if the tab is not visible.

To select a particular layer:

- Click a layer name in the Layers tab.

To add a new layer:

- In the Layers tab, click the 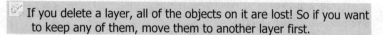 **Add Layer** button to add a new layer above the currently selected layer.

To rename a layer:

- To rename a layer to something more meaningful, click on the selected layer's name and type to add your new name (you can also make an insertion point to edit the existing text). A good example would be to rename the initial Layer 1 to be called "Background" (see above).

To delete a layer:

- In the Layers tab, select the layer's name and click the ▬ **Delete Layer** button.

If you delete a layer, all of the objects on it are lost! So if you want to keep any of them, move them to another layer first.

You can move layers up or down in the stacking order to place their objects in front or behind those on other layers, move objects to specific layers, and even merge layers.

To move a layer in the stacking order:

- ▲ ▼ In the Layers tab, select the layer's entry, then click the **Move Layer Up** or **Move Layer Down** button to move the layer up or down in the list, respectively.
  OR

- Drag the selected layer to a new position in the frame stack.

Remember that objects on layers are drawn in the order in which the layers were initially added to the Layers tab. Put another way: the bottom layer in the Layers tab stack is drawn first then the second bottom, third bottom etc. A background layer should be the bottom layer in the Layers tab stack.

The standard object ordering commands (Forward One, Back One, etc.) can be used on a layer, affecting an object's level within the layer it currently occupies. For more information, see **Ordering Objects** on p. 133.

At some point you may be confident that objects on separate layers can be managed on the same layer without compromising layer control. Merging layers enables this and will help to keep your layer management simpler. This rationalization is possible via the **Merge** button.

To merge a layer:

1. Activate the layer you want to merge **to** by clicking its entry. The layer is highlighted in blue. (Note that the active layer becomes uppermost in the workspace.)

2. With the **Ctrl** key pressed, select a single or multiple layers that you want to merge into the activated layer (the layers are framed with a blue border).

3. Click the **Merge** button. The contents of the merged layer(s) appear on the active layer and the previously selected layers disappear.

If you're working on an especially complex document you can temporarily freeze a layer (and its objects) once finished with to speed up performance. The layer is rasterized to a user-defined DPI (96 DPI by default) and is not editable until it is unfrozen (although it remains visible).

To freeze/unfreeze a layer:

- Right-click the layer and select **Freeze** from the flyout menu.
  OR
  Double-click the layer's thumbnail and, from the **Layer Properties** dialog, check **Freeze Layer** (optionally you can alter the DPI setting from the accompanying drop-down menu or slider).

Either method will display a snowflake (replacing the lock icon) at the end of the "frozen" layer's entry. Click the snowflake to unfreeze the layer.

If you're not ready to freeze a whole layer and all its objects you can freeze one or more selected objects instead. (See **Managing objects on layers** on p. 138).

Layer Properties

Layer properties allow you to assign paper textures, make layers invisible, non-printable and/or locked. An object's selection handle colour can also be defined based on its current layer. You can perform these operations directly from the Layers tab (or by double-clicking or right-click on a layer entry):

- Click the **Paper textures** icon to apply a texture to object(s) on a layer. The displayed dialog, offers a Paper Textures category from which you can choose a texture from a selection of texture thumbnails.

- Click/unclick the **Visible** icon to show/hide the layer and any objects on it.

- Click/unclick the 🖨 **Printable** icon to include/exclude the layer in printouts. This also means that the layer is not shown during **Publishing as PDF** or **Exporting** operations. Non-printing layers are handy "for information only."
  Note: Layers not checked as visible will still print, as long as they are checked as printable.

- Click/unclick the 🔒 **Locked** column to allow/prevent objects on the layer from being moved, deleted, or resized. (Clicking 🔒 on the Layer's entry locks the layer, which will then shown as 🔒).

- To set a Selection colour, double-click the layer's preview thumbnail preceding the layer name. From the dialog, click the colour swatch (e.g., 🔵) and choose a colour from the palette (click **More Colours...** for a wider choice). Assigning different colours to layers means that you can quickly verify that a pasted object has gone to the correct layer, i.e. the box surrounding the object on a layer always adopts the Selection colour assigned to the layer. The layer shows its current selection colour as a thin colour strip under the layer property icons.

Managing objects on layers

A useful feature of the Layers tab is that you can see objects or even groups of objects, under the layer on which they were created. This gives you the option of selecting an object or group from the tab as opposed to from the page itself. Either group or object can be named, and once named, the Find Objects option on the Edit menu easily locates a named object or group, selecting it in the process.

To add objects to a particular layer:

- When drawn, objects are added to the selected layer automatically. This is why it is a good idea to check which layer you are currently working on!

You can select objects subsequent to this either directly on the page or via the Layers tab. For the latter method, each layer entry can display an expanded **hierarchical tree view** of associated objects (along with thumbnail previews of each object) if objects have been created on the layer. This tree view greatly improves the ability to select and manage nested objects in more complex drawings. It's also great for visualizing your object order.

To select objects on a particular layer:

- In the Layers tab, if the 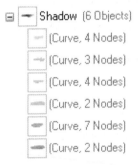 **Edit All Layers** button is disabled, click the chosen layer and either:

    - Click the layer's object on the page.
    OR

    - In the Layers tab, click the ⊞ Expand icon on the chosen layer entry to reveal all associated objects. You'll see objects named automatically, e.g. "Curve, 2 Nodes", "Closed Curve, 5 Nodes", "Quick Rectangle", etc., each with their own preview. The front most object in your drawing always appears at the top of the layer's listed objects (the order reflects the Z-order).

    ⊟ ━ Shadow (6 Objects)
          ═ (Curve, 4 Nodes)
          ━ (Curve, 3 Nodes)
          ═ (Curve, 4 Nodes)
          ▬ (Curve, 2 Nodes)
          ▬ (Curve, 7 Nodes)
          ▬ (Curve, 2 Nodes)

    To help you locate objects more easily in the future, they can be renamed (click and type on the name) to something more meaningful, and can be further identified by their thumbnail previews. Objects can also be searched for via **Find Objects...** on the Edit menu (see **Finding objects** on p. 124).

The object on the page is selected when selection handles appear on the object and the displayed bounding box reflects the selected layer's colour.

To select any object on any layer:

Initially, objects which are on layers that are not selected are also visible, but you may find that you can't select an object as it is on a different layer. This can be slightly confusing at first as you frantically click on an object to no effect! But of course, you can change this state of affairs.

- If ![icon] **View All Layers** is enabled (the default), all layers set as visible appear in the edit window, regardless of which layer you're currently working on. Disabling this button lets you see only objects on the current layer, as long as it's visible. (If both **Visible** and **View All Layers** are unchecked, you won't see anything!)

- If ![icon] **Edit All Layers** (available only if **View All Layers** is enabled) is disabled (the default), you can only select objects in the current layer. Enabling this button lets you select any object on any visible layer. You can press the Tab key repeatedly to cycle between objects in order.

- If ![icon] **Auto-Select Layer** is enabled (available only if **Edit All Layers** is enabled), you'll automatically select an object's layer and the object entry in the Layers tab as you select it on the page. This stops you from having to jump back to the Layers tab to set the layer to be active after object selection.

To change an object's or group's name:

1. In the Layers tab, expand the layer entry to which an object or group belongs.

2. Select the object/group, then click on its name.

3. At the insertion point, type a new name then either press Enter or click away from the tab.

> Trouble locating your **named** object or group? Search for it by using **Find Objects...** on the Edit menu. (see **Finding objects** on p. 124).

To move an object to another layer:

- Select the object, right-click and choose **Move Object to Layer...**. From the dialog, select the specific destination layer.
  OR

- Select the object, right-click and choose **Move Object to Active Layer**. The object moves to whichever layer was previously active.

To freeze any object on any layer:

- Select an object (or multiple objects with the **Ctrl** key), right-click and select **Freeze**. To unfreeze, click the ❄ snowflake displayed at the end of its object entry.

Like frozen layers, frozen objects are not editable.

8

Fill, Lines, Colours, and Transparency

Setting fill properties

Any closed shape, such as a closed curve or QuickShape, or text has an interior region that can be filled. The fill type can be solid, gradient, bitmap or plasma. Those that use a single colour are solid fills. Let's take a moment to run through them, using a plain old square as an example object.

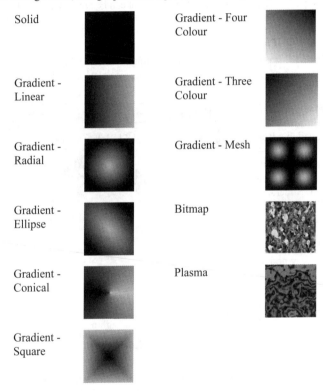

Solid	Gradient - Four Colour	
Gradient - Linear	Gradient - Three Colour	
Gradient - Radial	Gradient - Mesh	
Gradient - Ellipse	Bitmap	
Gradient - Conical	Plasma	
Gradient - Square		

Fill types fall into several basic categories:

- **Solid fills**, as their name implies, use a single colour.

- **Gradient fills** provide a gradation or spectrum of colours between two or more "key" colours. **Mesh fills** work like gradient fills but with a more complex fill path.

- **Bitmap and Plasma fills** apply bitmapped images or patterns to the object, each with unique properties. Think of Bitmap fills as named "pictures" that fill shapes. Plasma (or "fractal") fills use randomized patterns, useful for simulating cloud or shadow effects.

In DrawPlus, fills can use an unlimited combination of colours from a number of colour models. The Colour tab and Swatches tab displays swatches for all fill types which accurately represents the fill that can be applied. Navigate around the tabs and select as appropriate!

Solid colours

Applying a fill is easy, whether you're selecting a custom colour from the Colour tab or a preset colour from a whole range of colour swatches in the Swatches tab.

The **Colour tab** can operate in several modes available from a drop-down menu— HSL Colour Wheel (shown), HSL Colour Box, HSL Sliders, RGB Sliders, CMYK Sliders and Tinting. We'll concentrate on the HSL Colour Wheel which is very popular amongst drawing professionals.

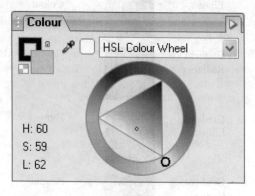

The HSL Colour Wheel is made up of three key components—the line/fill swatches, the outer Hue wheel and the Saturation/Lightness triangle.

The Line/Fill swatches govern whether the selected colour is applied as a line colour, solid fill, or both simultaneously.

The small circles shown in the wheel and triangle indicate the current setting for hue and saturation/lightness, respectively. Drag either circle around to adjust the overall HSL value.

A **Tinting** option in the Colour tab's drop-down menu (not shown above) allows a percentage of shade/tint to be applied to your colour.

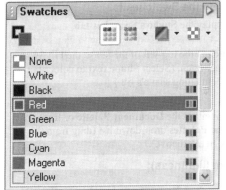

By comparison, the Swatches tab hosts a vast array of colour swatches for solid colour, gradient, plasma and bitmap fills.

To apply a solid fill colour via the Colour tab:

1. Select the object(s) and display the Studio's **Colour tab**.

2. Set the Line/Fill Swatch at the top-left of the tab so the Fill Swatch appears in front of the Line swatch. This defines where the colour will be applied. Alternatively, apply colour to both line and fill simultaneously by clicking the **Link** on the swatch.

3. Choose a colour display mode (HSL Colour Wheel, HSL Colour Box, HSL Sliders, RGB Sliders, or CMYK Sliders) from the drop-down menu.

4. Select a colour from the display.

Exact colour values can be set in a **Colour Selector** dialog available by either double-clicking the swatch or from **Format>Fill...**.

> When setting no fill, the Saturation/Lightness triangle disappears on the Colour tab's HSL Colour Wheel as colour is no longer set.

To apply a solid fill colour via the Swatches tab:

1. Select the object(s) and display the Studio's **Swatches tab**.

2. Set the Line/Fill Swatch at the top-left of the tab so the Fill Swatch appears in front of the Line swatch. (Select **Shape text** to colour the characters rather than the containing shape's fill.)

3. ick a thumbnail from either the **Document Palette** or from another palette shown in the **Palettes** drop-down list (drag from the thumbnail onto the line as an alternative).

To change a fill's shade/tint (lightness):

1. Select the object and set the Line/Fill Swatch as described for the Colour tab above.

2. From the tab's drop-down menu, select **Tinting**.

3. Drag the **Shade/Tint** slider to the left or right to darken or lighten your starting colour, respectively (the original colour is set at 0%). You can also enter a percentage value in the box (entering 0 or dragging the pointer back to its original position reverts to the original colour).

To apply a gradient, Bitmap, or Plasma fill to one or more objects:

As for applying a solid colour fill with the Swatches tab but:

- Instead of using a solid colour palette, pick a relevant category from the **Gradient** or **Bitmap** galleries, and pick your required thumbnail from the displayed presets (drag from the thumbnail onto the object as an alternative).

For solid, gradient or Plasma fills, you can then edit **colour(s) and shade/tint** (lightness). For gradient and plasma fills, the fill **path** (coverage) can also be edited (see **Working with Gradient Fills** on p. 158).

To edit an object's fill colour(s) and tint:

1. Right-click the object and choose **Format>Fill...** (or choose the command from the Format menu).

2. Use the vertical slider to the immediate right of the colour space window to set your colour value (or use the Input box).

3. Click anywhere in the colour space window then drag the marker around to fine-tune your colour selection.

To adjust a non-solid fill's path:

- Click the ⬦ **Fill Tool** button on the Drawing toolbar and drag the fill's nodes.

To apply a transparent fill:

Set a transparent interior for objects by using the:

- **Colour tab**: Click ⬛ **No Fill** in the bottom-left corner of the Line/Fill Swatch (Colour tab), which represents either None (a transparent interior for objects with line/fill properties) or Original (for pictures only, to reset the object to its original colours). See **Using transparency effects** on p. 165.
  OR

- **Swatches tab**: Choose the first swatch, ⬛ **None**, from any gallery.

> When setting no fill, the Saturation/Lightness triangle disappears on the Colour tab's HSL Colour Wheel as colour is no longer set.

Setting the default fill

See the topic **Updating defaults** on p. 43.

Setting line properties

Lines, curves, and shapes are all variations of one basic object: the line. They all consist of one or more line segments drawn between junction points called nodes. In general, if we use the word "line" it can mean either a straight line or a curve. A shape is a line whose ends have been connected to form an enclosed region.

Line art offers an unlimited opportunity to draw not only the basic line, but many other curves and object borders which are considered line based. A vast array of effects and tools can be applied such that you are limited only by your imagination. Consider a few interesting types of line art ...all possible from within DrawPlus.

All lines, including those that enclose shapes, have numerous properties, including colour, weight (width or thickness), scaling, cap (end), and join (corner).

Using the Studio's Line tab, you can adjust **plain line** properties for any freeform, straight, or curved line, as well as for the outline of a shape.

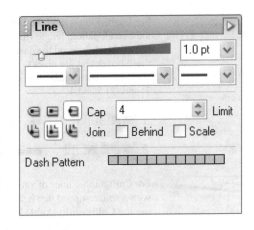

If needed, any line can be saved for future use in a Line Styles tab. Either add to the **Plain** category or your own named category by clicking the **Add line to current category** button when your line is selected.

In addition to plain lines, the Line Styles tab offers many categories of decorative **chain lines** (also known as picture tubes) which use repeating bitmap elements strung along the length of the line. (See **Creating chain lines** on p. 163).

For details on adding or editing plain line colours, see **Defining solid line and fill colours** on p. 153.

To set properties of a plain line:

1. To set line weight (width) , drag the top slider in the Line tab, select a value from the drop-down list, or enter a value directly. To turn off the line, set the box to 0.0pt.

2. To set other line properties, make separate selections for Line Start, Line Style, and Line End from the drop-down lists.
   For the Line Style drop-down menu, you can choose **None**, **Single**, **Dashed**, **Double**, or **Calligraphic** styles.

Several styles provide additional ways to customize the line:

For Dashed lines, drag the **Dash Pattern** slider to set the overall pattern length (the number of boxes to the left of the slider) and the dash length (the number of those boxes that are black). The illustrations below show lines with pattern and dash lengths of (**1**) 4 and 2; and (**2**) 5 and 4:

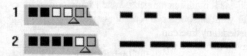

For Calligraphic lines of variable width (drawn as if with a square-tipped pen held at a certain angle), use the **Calligraphy Angle** box to set the angle of the pen tip, as depicted in the adjacent box.

The Line tab also lets you vary a line's **Cap** (end) and the **Join** (corner) where two lines intersect. Both properties tend to be more conspicuous on thicker lines; joins are more apparent with more acute angles. The respective button icons clearly communicate each setting:

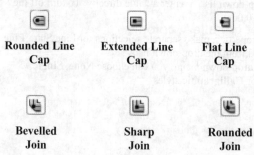

Rounded Line Cap   **Extended Line Cap**   **Flat Line Cap**

Bevelled Join   **Sharp Join**   **Rounded Join**

The ☑ Behind check box controls line width relative to object size—useful with very small objects or when resizing text. When checked, the object's line appears behind its fill; otherwise, the whole line appears in front of the line.

Check the ☑ Scale check box to automatically expand and contract the line thickness in proportion to the object size (or uncheck to make the line's thickness remain unchanged). When scaling text, for example, you might either want the border to remain the same width, or change in proportion to the overall characters.

You can use a variety of methods to set a plain line's colour and fine-tune its colour overall tint (lightness). You can use the Colour or Swatches tab to define the line colour or shade/tint as described in **Setting fill properties** on p. 145. You'll need to set the Line swatch accordingly (e.g., ◼).

Defining solid line and fill colours

When you're applying a **solid fill** or **line colour** using the Studio's **Swatches tab**, you choose a colour from one of several colour **palettes**, arranged as a gallery of colour swatch thumbnails. Different palettes can be loaded but only one palette is displayed at any one time. Several of the colour palettes are based on "themed" colours while the remaining palettes are based on industry-standard colour models, i.e.

- **RGB**: Red, Green and Blue (default)
- **CMYK**: Cyan, Magenta, Yellow and Black

Palettes can be loaded, created, deleted and saved as discussed later in **Managing colours and palettes** on p. 155.

Changing the set of gallery colours

Colours are added manually or automatically from the Colour tab or taken directly from a drawing object's line/fill into the user's **Document Palette**. The palette also stores commonly used colours (e.g., Red, Green, Blue, etc.). Once a colour is stored in the Document Palette, it can be edited with the Colour Selector dialog at any time. Colours can be added, edited, deleted, or renamed within the Document Palette as in any of the other Swatches tab's palettes.

To add a colour to the Document Palette:

1. Either:

- Select a colour mixed from the Colour tab.

OR:

1. Use the ✐ ◼ **Colour Picker** on the Colour tab to select any colour already on your page. Click on the dropper icon (hold down the mouse button for magnification) and select your chosen pickup colour with the pickup cursor. The colour is picked up in the **Picked Colour** swatch.

2. Click this swatch to transfer the colour to the **Fill** swatch.

2. Click the ▷ **Tab Menu** button on the Colour tab.

3. If **Automatically Add to Document Palette** is checked, the colour is added immediately—if unchecked, click **Add to palette** to add it manually.

If the colour doesn't already exist in the Swatches tab's Document Palette, a new thumbnail appears for it.

To add an object's solid colour line or fill to the Document Palette:

1. Select the object, and set the Swatches tab's **Line** or **Fill** swatch, depending on which attribute's solid colour you want to add.

2. Right-click the object and choose **Add to Studio>Fill...** (or choose from the Format menu). A new thumbnail appears at the bottom of the Document Palette.

If the colour doesn't already exist in the Document Palette, a new thumbnail appears for it. To add text colours to the gallery, add the colour as you would for a fill colour.

To add a new gallery colour:

1. Display the **Document Palette** from the Swatches tab.

2. Right-click any solid colour thumbnail and choose **Add...**.

3. From the Colour Selector dialog, click on a new position in the colour space window to set a new colour. Alternatively, enter values in the adjacent input boxes.

4. Click **OK**. Scroll to the bottom of the gallery to see your new thumbnail. A new thumbnail is immediately added at the bottom of the Document Palette.

You can also define a new gallery colour while editing an object's line or fill, as described below. Click the Colour Selector's Add to Palette button.

To redefine an existing gallery colour:

1. Right-click a sample in any palette (Swatches tab) and choose **Edit...**.

2. Choose a different colour from the colour spectrum in the **Colour Selector** dialog.

3. Click the **OK** button. The colour and its thumbnail are permanently updated.

To delete a gallery colour:

- Right-click its solid colour thumbnail in any palette (Swatches tab) and choose **Delete**.

If any existing objects use a colour, if you delete it, the objects will retain it, but only as a local (object) fill.

You can also change the definition of any preset colour or fill that appears in the Swatches tab. The process is comparable to adjusting an object's "local" fill, but your change will be permanently available as an updated gallery thumbnail for future use.

Managing colours and palettes

DrawPlus ships with a varied selection of **palettes**, stored separately as .PLT files. The RGB and CMYK palettes can be loaded, along with other "themed" palettes including Earth, Pastels, and Soft Tones. The "themed" palettes offer an alternative to using the RGB and CMYK palettes. Palettes can also be created, deleted and, for the Document Palette, saved.

Colours in the Document palette (as shown in the Swatches tab) are just saved locally, along with the drawing's current defaults. That is, the colours don't automatically carry over to new drawings. However changes to the other palettes are saved globally, in that colour changes will carry over to new documents automatically.

To load a named palette:

1. In the Swatches tab, click the down arrow on the **Palettes** button.

2. From the resulting drop-down menu, select an Standard RGB, Standard CMYK, or "themed" palette, or a palette that you've created yourself.

The loaded palette's colours appear as swatches in the Swatches tab, replacing the swatches previously visible.

To create a new custom palette:

1. With the **Palettes** button selected in the Swatches tab, click the ▷ **Tab Menu** button in the tab's top right-hand corner and choose **Add New Palette...**.

2. Enter a name for the new palette and click **OK**. The new empty palette is displayed and its name will appear in the Palettes drop-down menu.

To delete a new custom palette:

1. In the Swatches tab, select the palette for deletion from the **Palettes** drop-down list.

2. Click the ▷ **Tab Menu** button in the top right-hand corner and choose **Delete Palette...**. After confirmation, the palette is removed from the list.

To save the Document Palette: :saving

1. Right-click on any colour thumbnail in the Document Palette and choose **Palette Manager**.

2. In the dialog, choose the **Options** button pick **Save Palette As...** and save the palette to a new .PLT file.

> If you store the file in another folder to the initially prompted one, then your saved palette will not appear in the **Palettes** drop-down menu.

Linked colours

A **linked colour** is a colour you define as a shade/tint of any existing solid colour (the "**base colour**") created in the Studio's Swatches tab. You can use linked colours just like regular solid colours to fill objects throughout your drawing. Since the colours are linked back to the base colour, if you want to update all linked colours, you simply modify the base colour.

Typically, you'll firstly create a base colour (with a unique name of your choosing), then create linked colours as shades of that base colour.

To create a linked base colour:

1. In any palette on the Studio's Swatches tab, right-click and choose **Add Linked...**.
   OR

   In the Colour tab, select the ▷ **Tab Menu** button and choose **Add to Palette (Linked)**.

2. In the Colour Selector dialog, select a base colour from the window (i.e., the colour that all object colours will link to). A thumbnail will appear at the end of the palette.

If you're working with already drawn objects, save your object's fill as a linked base colour by right-clicking and choosing **Format >Fill**. The dialog's **Options** button allows you to **Add to Palette (Linked)**.

The thumbnails of a linked base colour and a standard solid colour differ—the former displays a small tab in its bottom-right corner (i.e., ◩ compared to ▪). Linked colour presets are also named as Linked Red, Linked Green, etc.

To apply linked colours to an object:

1. Apply a linked base colour to a specific or multiple object's fill, line or text.

2. In the Colour tab, display the **Tinting** option in the drop-down menu.

3. Select objects one by one, each time applying a different percentage shade/tint—drag the **Shade/Tint** slider to change the shading.

Instead of your objects being filled independently a linkage now exists to the same base colour. A simple update of the base colour updates all objects automatically.

> The **Tinting** option shows the base colour from which an object's colour is derived.

To update linked colours:

1. In the Swatches tab, right-click the base colour's thumbnail and choose **Edit...**.

2. Use the Colour Selector dialog to define a new colour value.

3. Click **OK**. The gallery thumbnail, and any drawn objects (on any layer or page) using the linked colours, are updated immediately.

TIP: Use **Format Painter** on the Standard toolbar to apply linked colours between objects on the page.

Working with gradient fills

Gradient fills are those that use gradients—small "spectrums" with colours spreading between at least two defined **key** values. Specifically, gradient fills include the **Linear**, **Radial**, **Ellipse**, **Conical**, **Square**, **Three Colour**, and **Four Colour** types. Once you've applied a gradient fill to an object using the Swatches tab (see **Setting fill properties** on p. 145), you can use the **Fill Tool** to edit the object's **fill path**, defining the placement of the spectrum across the object.

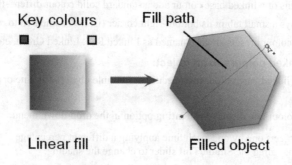

Key colours ■ □   Fill path

Linear fill   Filled object

Applying a gradient fill

There are several ways to apply a gradient fill as a line colour or object fill: using the Fill Tool or via the Swatches tab. Using the Fill Tool, you can vary the fill's path on an object for different effects.

To apply a gradient fill (Fill Tool):

1. Select a coloured object.

2. Click the ⬥ **Fill Tool** button on the Drawing toolbar.

3. Click and drag on the object to define the fill path (a solid line). The object takes a simple Linear fill, grading from the current colour of the object, ending in white (objects filled with white will grade from white to black, to show contrast).

To apply a gradient fill (Swatches tab):

1. Select an object.

2. Click the Swatches tab and ensure the **Fill** swatch is placed in front of Line swatch.

3. For gradient fills, select the ⬛▾ **Gradient** button's drop-down menu and pick a gradient category.

4. Click the thumbnail for the fill you want to apply.
    OR
    Drag from the gallery swatch onto any object.

Editing the fill path

If an object using a gradient fill is selected, you'll see the **fill path** displayed as one or more lines, with circular nodes marking where the spectrum between each key colour begins and ends. Adjusting the node positions determines the actual spread of colours between nodes. You can also edit the fill by adding, deleting, or changing key colours.

To adjust the gradient fill path on a selected object:

1. Select an object with a gradient fill.

2. Click the ◆ **Fill Tool** button on the Drawing toolbar. The object's fill path appears.

3. Use the Fill Tool to drag the start and end circular path nodes, or drag on (or outside) the object for a new start node, creating a new fill path as you drag. The gradient starts where you place the start node, and ends where you place the end node.

4.   To constrain the fill path in 15-degree increments, hold down the **Shift** key while dragging. On Ellipse fills, **Ctrl**-constraining also forces the gradient's aspect ratio to match the object's bounding box.

Each gradient fill type has a characteristic path. For example, Radial fills have single-line paths, with the gradient initially starting at the object's centre. Ellipse fills likewise begin at the centre, but their paths have two lines so you can adjust the fill's extent in two directions away from the centre. Radial fills are always evenly circular, while Ellipse fills can be skewed in one direction or another.

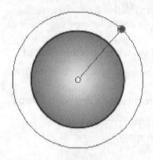   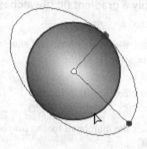

Radial Fill   **Ellipse Fill**

Experiment to discover new effects! For example, you can widen or narrow the gradient's extent, even drag either node completely outside the object. Or, for Radial and Ellipse fills on a round shape, try placing the start node near the figure's upper edge, off-centre, to create a reflection highlight.

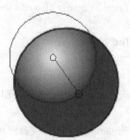

For details of how to edit and manage gradient fills, see DrawPlus help.

Editing the fill spectrum

Whether you're editing a fill that's been already been applied to an object, or redefining one of the gallery fills, the basic concepts are the same. Whereas solid fills use a single colour, all gradient fills utilize at least two "key" colours, with a spread of hues in between each key colour, creating a "spectrum" effect.

You can either edit the fill spectrum directly using the **Fill Tool** or use **Format>Fill** (to access the Gradient Fill Editor dialog). With the Fill Tool selected, colours can be selected from the Studio's Colour or Swatches tab to replace a selected node's colour, or dragged from the Swatches tab to create new nodes on the fill path). Both methods let you define key colours. The Fill Tool method is more convenient for this, but with the dialog you can also fine-tune the actual spread of colour between pairs of key colours.

The editing of gradient fills is a complex operation and is covered in greater detail in the DrawPlus help.

Working with Bitmap and Plasma fills

A **Bitmap fill** uses a named bitmap—often a material, pattern, or background image. DrawPlus supplies an impressive selection of preset Bitmap fills on the Swatches tab, and you can import your own.

A **Plasma fill**, sometimes called a fractal fill, is a bitmapped pattern with dark and light regions, useful for simulating cloud or shadow effects. Again, the Swatches tab hosts a selection of these fills.

Once you've applied either type of fill to an object using the Swatches tab (see **Setting fill properties** on p. 145), you can adjust the fill's tint with the Shade/Tint slider in the Colour tab (use Display mode drop-down menu), and use the Fill Tool to edit the object's **fill path**, defining the placement of the fill across the object.

Editing the fill path

If an object using a bitmap fill is selected, you'll see the **fill path** displayed as two lines joined at a Centre handle. Nodes, shown as small filled circles, mark the fill's centre and edges.

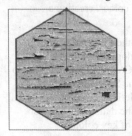

To reposition the fill's centre, drag the centre handle. To create a skewed or tilted fill region, drag one or both edge nodes sideways.

Unlike the other fill types, Bitmap and Plasma fills don't simply "end" at the edges of their fill path. Rather, they **tile** (repeat) so you can fill indefinitely large regions at any scale. By dragging the edge nodes in or out with the Fill Tool, you can "zoom" in or out on the fill pattern.

For details of how to edit and manage Bitmap and Plasma fills, see DrawPlus help.

Changing the set of Bitmap gallery fills

The Bitmap gallery on the Swatches tab provides a large selection of bitmaps, grouped into categories like Abstract, Material, Patterns, and so on. The existing categories are already populated with preset swatches, but initially, there's one category ("My Bitmaps") that's empty and reserved for your own bitmaps. You can add more categories, and add bitmaps to them either by importing directly from a file or by adopting the bitmap fill of an object on the DrawPlus page.

Changing the set of Plasma gallery fills

If you've defined a new Plasma fill on an object, you can add it to the set of gallery fills shown on the Swatches tab so that it will be available to use again. In addition, you can delete, redefine, or rename any Plasma gallery fill.

For more information on changing both Bitmap and Plasma fills, see DrawPlus help.

Working with Mesh fills

A **Mesh fill** works like a gradient fill but uses a more complex fill path, with a grid or "mesh" of many nodes representing separate key colours. The overall effect, especially useful for multifaceted highlighting, arises from the colour gradients that spread between each of these nodes.

The mesh fill is shown below when the object is unselected (left) or when the Fill Tool active (right); when active the tool enables the mesh of nodes to be displayed and edited.

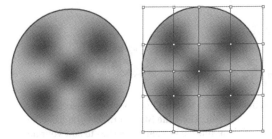

A Mesh fill is applied to an object via the Swatches tab's Gradient gallery (see **Setting fill properties** on p. 145). You can edit the mesh itself with the **Mesh Fill Tool** and the accompanying context toolbar to achieve unique results. The path lines that connect nodes in a Mesh fill are actually curves, so editing the mesh is similar to the method for Editing lines and shapes (see p. 57). Simple warping effects, colour spread changes and path line curvature can all be affected. The tool lets you reshape curved path lines by adjusting one or more nodes and their control handles. In addition, the area between four nodes called "mesh patches" can be recoloured or moved individually or in multiples. As for curved lines you can add, delete, and move one or more nodes at any time.

For full details of how to edit and manage Mesh fills, see DrawPlus help.

Creating chain lines

A **chain** (or **chain line**) is a decorative line incorporating one or more individual DrawPlus objects arrayed along its length—rather like a **border** motif, but with all the freeform adaptability of a plain line.

Chains are constructed by "stringing together" one or more objects, adding one selection at a time to the chain. The **Line Styles tab** lets you can choose from a wide assortment of chain lines, edit their properties to suit your needs, or create your own chains from scratch. Apply chains to lines, curves, QuickShapes, filled shapes, even text... anywhere you want to instantly introduce repeating elements.

To apply a chain line:

1. Switch on the Studio's **Line Styles** tab from the **Studio Tabs** option on the View menu. The tab is switched off by default.

2. Select a chain line category (all except "Plain") from the drop-down menu.

3. Choose and drag your chain line thumbnail onto an object (or select the object first, then click the thumbnail).

While the pre-supplied chains in the gallery offer plenty of possibilities, it's quite easy to create your own by "stringing together" one or more DrawPlus objects, adding one selection at a time to the chain.

You can create your own chain line or edit a preset chain line, but as a more advanced subject, this is dealt with in DrawPlus help.

Using transparency

Transparency effects are great for highlights, shading and shadows, and simulating "rendered" realism. They can make the critical difference between flat-looking illustrations and images with depth and snap.

Transparency may seem a bit tricky because by definition, you can't "see" it the way you can see a colour fill applied to an object. In fact, it's there all the time in DrawPlus. Each new object has a transparency property: the default just happens to be "None"—that is, no transparency (opaque).

Transparencies work rather like fills that use "disappearing ink" instead of colour. The more transparency in a particular spot, the more "disappearing" takes place there, and the more the object(s) underneath show through. Just as a gradient fill can vary from light to dark, a transparency can vary from more to less, i.e. from clear to opaque, as in the illustration:

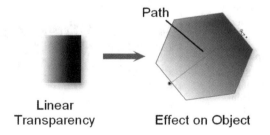

**Linear
Transparency**   **Effect on Object**

Here, the hexagonal shape has had a Linear transparency applied, with more transparency at the lower end of the transparency **path** and less at the upper end.

In DrawPlus, transparency effects work very much like greyscale fills, in that they can be applied along an editable path, and they can be applied as a custom transparency or from a range of preset thumbnails. Another similarity is that all transparency effect names are comparable to the fills of the same name, i.e. solid, gradient and bitmap transparencies are available.

- **Solid** transparency distributes the transparency equally across the object.

- **Gradient** transparencies include **Linear**, **Radial**, **Ellipse**, **Conical**, **Plasma**, **Square**, **Three Points** and **Four Points** (each thumbnail's tooltip identifies its category), ranging from clear to opaque.

- The **Bitmap** transparency gallery host texture maps based on the Swatches tab's selection of bitmaps.

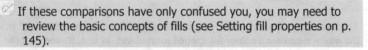 If these comparisons have only confused you, you may need to review the basic concepts of fills (see Setting fill properties on p. 145).

Applying transparency

There are two ways to apply transparency, i.e. via the:

- Transparency tab
- Transparency Tool

Let's check out the Transparency tab. As with the Swatches tab, there are galleries for solid, gradient and bitmap transparencies.

Each preset's tooltip is expressed in percentage Opacity, an attribute of the Transparency effect. Think of this as the inverse of transparency—100% Opacity = 0% Transparency and vice versa.

For objects with Gradient transparencies (Linear, Radial, Ellipse, etc.) you can adjust the transparency effect by adding or subtracting nodes from the gradient transparency path, which closely resemble those of their fill counterparts. The Transparency Tool can display an object's gradient transparency, indicated by two or more nodes situated along a path. You can reposition the nodes to adjust the transparency's starting point or end point, or if more than two nodes are present, intermediate levels of transparency along the path.

For transparencies with multiple nodes, each node has its own value, comparable to a key colour in a gradient fill. Each node value can be altered directly on the page (click a sample thumbnail to apply the edit), by using the Gradient Transparency Editor dialog or the Transparency tab. The dialog offers more precise control over more complex gradient transparencies.

To apply transparency with Transparency tab:

1. With your object selected, go to the Transparency tab.

2. For solid transparency, select the 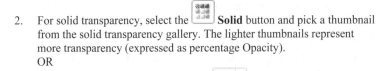 **Solid** button and pick a thumbnail from the solid transparency gallery. The lighter thumbnails represent more transparency (expressed as percentage Opacity).
   OR

   For gradient transparency, choose the **Gradient** button and pick your thumbnail from a range of categories.
   OR

   For Bitmap transparency, choose the **Bitmap** button and pick a thumbnail from a range of categories.

3. The transparency is applied to the object(s).

> Sometimes objects of a lighter colour will not display their transparency clearly—ensure the transparency is applied correctly by temporarily placing the object over a strong solid colour.

Alternatively, drag the desired thumbnail from the gallery to an object (the cursor changes to include a plus sign over suitable objects), and release the mouse button. The object takes the transparency and becomes the selected object.

To apply gradient transparency with Transparency Tool:

1. Select an object.

2. Click the [icon] **Transparency Tool** button on the Drawing toolbar.

3. Click and drag on the object to define the transparency path. The object takes a simple Linear transparency, grading from 100% opacity to 0% opacity.

Editing a transparency effect applied to an object is actually simpler than editing a fill, because the concept of "colour" doesn't exist in transparency. When adjusting a transparency effect that's been applied to an object, you don't have to worry about editing a colour gradient—only tweaking the path and (for Solid transparencies) varying the level of transparency with a slider.

Once you've applied a transparency, you can adjust its **path** on the object, and the **level** of transparency along the path. You can even create more complex transparency effects by adding extra nodes to the path and assigning different levels to each node.

To adjust the transparency path:

- Use the tool to drag individual nodes, or click on the object for a new start node and drag out a new transparency path. The effect starts where you place the start node, and ends where you place the end node. For Bitmap and Plasma transparencies, the path determines the centre and two edges of the effect.

Editing a **gradient transparency** path is similar to editing a comparable **fill path**. Adding a level of transparency means varying the transparency gradient by introducing a new **node** and assigning it a particular value. For transparencies with multiple nodes, each node has its own value, comparable to a key colour in a gradient fill. Note that you cannot alter the values in a Bitmap transparency.

You can either edit the path directly using the **Transparency Tool** in conjunction with the Transparency tab, or use the **Gradient Transparency Editor** dialog exclusively (this is similar to the Gradient Fill Editor). Both methods let you define key values along the path.

The dialog lets you fine-tune the actual spread of transparency between pairs of key values, and displays the transparency gradient, with pointers marking the nodes (corresponding to nodes on the path) that define specific transparency values. Again, black represents 100% opacity, and white represents 0% opacity, with greyscale values in between. A sample window at the lower right shows the overall transparency effect.

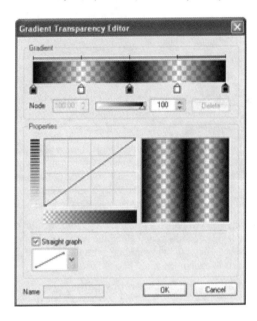

For details of how to edit and manage transparency, see DrawPlus help.

9

Animations

Getting started with animation

What is animation? Like flip books, Disney movies and TV, it's a way of creating the illusion of motion by displaying a series of still images, rapidly enough to fool the eye—or more accurately, the brain. Professional animators have developed a whole arsenal of techniques for character animation—rendering human (and animal) movement in a convincing way.

A clear distinction has to be made between two types of animation techniques, both possible from within DrawPlus, i.e.

- **Stopframe animation:** also known as Stop motion animation, involves the animation of static objects frame-by-frame. In the film industry, Stopframe animation is used within widely known productions based on figures made of clay or other bendable material (think King Kong!, and more recently Wallace & Gromit™ films (Aardman/Wallace and Gromit Ltd).

- **Keyframe animation:** performs movement of computer-generated objects from basic shapes to cartoon characters (used traditionally in Stopframe animation). Using the power of computing, spaces between key moments in your animation, defined by the user as **keyframes**, can be interleaved automatically with interpolated intermediate frames; creating a smooth and professional animation playback (compared to stopframe animation).

DrawPlus lets you **export** stopframe or keyframe animations to a variety of different formats. For more details, review **Exporting animations** (see p. 206).

For now we'll look at how to set up Stopframe or Keyframe animation mode within DrawPlus.

To begin a new Stopframe or Keyframe animation from scratch:

- Either select:

  - Choose **New>New Stopframe Animation** from the File menu. OR

  - Choose **New>New Keyframe Animation** from the File menu.

A new document window opens in the respective Animation mode.

To convert an existing drawing to either animation mode:

1. Choose **Convert to Stopframe Animation** or **Convert to Keyframe Animation** from the File menu. You'll be prompted to save changes (if any) to your existing drawing.

2. Select **Yes** to save your work, **No** to convert to an animation or **Cancel** to continue working on your current drawing.

To adjust the basic layout of your animation:

1. Choose **Page Setup** from the context toolbar (shown with Pointer or Rotate Tool selected).

2. Select a preset page type (e.g., Banner Ad) from the **Size** drop-down menu (or keep Custom selected, then set units for page width and height).

3. Choose **Wide** or **Tall** as the page orientation.

4. Choose values for left, right, top, and bottom **Margins**.

5. Click **OK**. Your page dimensions are expressed in pixels.

> You can modify page characteristics such as page size, orientation, number of pages, and snapping from the Pages context toolbar.

To save an animation:

- Choose **File>Save...**. DrawPlus saves animation documents in the proprietary .DPA format (Drawings are saved as .DPPs).

Working with Stopframe animation

The most important difference in Stopframe animation mode to the usual Drawing mode is that you'll be working predominantly with the **Frames tab**, ideally suited for animation because of its width and easy control of individual frames (stopframes are spread along the tab for easier management).

Use the Frames tab exclusively to insert, delete, clone or reorder frames, and access individual frame properties. DrawPlus's Hintline toolbar navigation buttons let you jump to the first, previous, next, and last frames as you would for normal documents. The tab also lets you preview the animation and enable **onion skinning** directly; exporting as a standalone animated GIF or video is carried out via the File menu.

The Frames tab is designed for Stopframe animation only, and only shows while in this mode. Don't get this tab confused with the Storyboard tab, used in the other type of animation supported by DrawPlus, **Keyframe animation** (see p. 173). Each tab hosts distinctly different tools suited to the respective animation type.

In most cases, your new Stopframe animation will have a single initial frame (e.g., Frame 1). To create new frames, you can either clone the current frame or insert a blank frame after the current frame. Choose to clone if you will be reusing the current frame's contents with a transformation of some kind (the most common way of simulating change or movement).

Try to think of your frame arrangement as a chronological sequence of static images which, when animated, will create the illusion of movement (like a cartoon flick-book). Once you've finished creating frames you can preview or export your animation, just as you would play the frames of a movie.

To view the Frames tab:

- Unless the tab is already displayed, click the ▬▬▲▬▬ handle at the bottom of your workspace to reveal the tab.

To clone the current frame to a new frame:

- Select a frame in the Frames tab, and choose [⊞ Clone Frame].

The frame is added after the selected frame.

> TIP: Alternatively, use the Blend Tool to automatically create "intermediate" stopframes in steps between objects. See **Stopframe animation tips and tricks** on p. 180.

To generate a new blank frame:

- Choose [⊞ Insert Frame] from the Frames tab.

Any new frame appears on the Frames tab to the right of existing frames, and then becomes the current frame.

To navigate between frames:

- Click on any visible frame to display its objects on screen (objects can then be edited).
  OR
  Click the **First**, **Previous**, **Next**, or **Last** navigation button on the Hintline toolbar to jump to start/end frame and navigate frame-by-frame.

To rename a frame:

- Click the frame's name under its frame thumbnail and type a new name.

To change frame sequence:

- Drag the selected frame to a new position in the frame order. When the dragged frame's thumbnail creates a slightly wider space between two frames than usual, release the mouse button to place the frame to be moved.

To delete a selected frame:

- Click ☒ Delete Frame from the Frames tab.

Onion Skinning

Onion skinning is a standard animation technique derived from cel animation, where transparent sheets enable the artist to see through to the preceding frame(s). It's useful for enabling precise registration and controlling object movement from frame to frame. You can turn the feature on or off (the default is off) as needed, and set the number of previous frames that will be visible (normally one).

To turn onion skinning on or off:

1. From the Frames tab, click the ☑ Onion Skinning button to turn onion skinning on or off.

2. (Optional) To set more than one previous frame to be visible, click **Properties**, then set the number of frames in the **Onion Skinning** input box.

The preceding frames' objects will show behind those of the currently selected frame.

Previewing Stopframe animations

You can **preview** your animation at any time either directly from your Frames tab (shown in a Preview window) or from within your default web browser. This is a quick way of checking it prior to export (for preview, DrawPlus exports a temporary version and loads it directly into the browser).

To preview in the Preview window:

- Click the 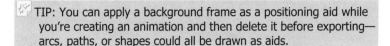 button on the Frames tab.

The animation loads into the Preview window and begins playing at its actual size and speed. Notice that you see only the drawn portion of the animation— any extra surrounding white space is cropped away. You can use the control buttons (Play, Stop, etc.) to review individual frames.

To preview in a web browser:

- For stopframe animation, select **Preview in Browser** from the File menu. The animation loads your default web browser and begins playing.

  This actually exports a temporary copy of the animation, using the current export settings and displays it in your Web browser. You can leave the browser open and DrawPlus will find it again next time you issue the command.

Using Background and Overlay frames

DrawPlus supports two methods of reusing elements across multiple frames: **Background frames** and **Overlay frames**.

Background frames

You can designate any frame as a **Background frame**, which remains visible while the following frames animate "over" it. Typically, this would be the first frame in your sequence—for example, a clock face that remained static while hands (on the following frames) revolved around the dial. A Background frame remains visible until any subsequent background frame is encountered; that second background frame is then carried forward, then the third, etc.

> TIP: You can apply a background frame as a positioning aid while you're creating an animation and then delete it before exporting— arcs, paths, or shapes could all be drawn as aids.

To create a Background frame:

- In the Frames tab, click on the ![icon] icon at the bottom of your chosen frame.
  OR

1. Right-click the chosen frame and choose **Properties...**.

2. From the dialog, enable the **Styles** radio button to be set to **Background**. Note that objects on the frame are now shown on all frames. Check the **Normal** radio button to revert the background frame to a normal frame again.

You'll see the objects on the background frame carried forward either to the end of the animation or to the next background frame.

Overlay frames

The main advantage of frame overlaying is to save you the time of having to copy or redraw objects in a series where each frame builds cumulatively on previous frames. The white portions of **Overlay frames** become "transparent," so the contents of the preceding frame show through. The effect is cumulative, so Overlays are most useful in a series where each frame builds on the contents of all the previous overlay frames. For example, you could show a series of footprints being laid down, starting with the first footprint in the first frame the second frame, and so on. Using Overlay frames, since all the footprints would remain visible, you wouldn't have to place more than one object in each frame. And of course, you can use Overlays in combination with a Background frame.

The Overlay effect resembles that of onion skinning (see **Working with Stopframe animation** on p. 174), but it's actually a frame property that becomes part of the final animation.

To make the current frame an Overlay frame:

- In the Frames tab, click on the ⬚ icon at the bottom of your chosen frame.
OR

1. Right-click the chosen frame and choose **Properties...**.

2. From the dialog, enable the **Styles** radio button to be set to **Overlay**.

3. Click **OK**. Objects drawn on the previous frame are now shown in the current frame (the previous frame can also be an overlay frame, showing the frames' objects previous to that, etc.). Check the **Normal** radio button to revert the overlay frame to a normal frame again.

Adjusting stopframe properties

You can set the frame duration—how long each frame displays—both globally and locally, and specify whether the animation plays as a continuous loop or repeats a certain number of times.

To set a global frame duration (same timing for each frame):

1. Select ⬚ Properties from the Frames tab.

2. Check the **Display each frame for** box and specify a duration setting (in milliseconds). Click **OK**.

Setting the frame timing globally in this way resets any individual frame timings you may have set. In general, set the global frame duration first, then go back and adjust individual frame timings as needed.

To set the duration of an individual frame:

- Click the frame's duration (e.g., 100ms) under its thumbnail, and, when selected, type a new value then click away.

To specify loop or repeat playback:

1. Select ⬚ Properties from the Frames tab.

2. Enable either **Loop continuously** (the default) or **Repeat animation for**, and set the number of repeated loops if needed.

Animation tips and tricks

QuickShape animation

The QuickShape flyout offers dozens of shapes, each with its own variations. The ease with which you can immediately alter QuickShapes makes them ideal starting points for geometric animation effects, whether used singly or in combination with text or other elements.

Remember that dragging the node handles of any QuickShape (see p. 64) provides an instant preview of many possible animation effects. By using this feature you can create frame sequences by cloning frames and adjusting the object as you go. Of course, you can vary the size and position of the QuickShape, too. In the example below, a Quick Clock shape can be animated by cloning each QuickShape while changing the minute hand of the clock face.

Text animation

So far we've dealt exclusively with QuickShape objects, but the same basic principles of positioning and timing apply to any object you want to animate, including text. As you may know from working with **Text** (see p. 93), DrawPlus gives you a wide choice of ways to vary text, ranging from simple size or fill changes to more complex effects like envelope distortions or blends. As with QuickShapes, any ways means by which you can vary an object's appearance can be put to good use in animation.

Almost any change you can apply to text has potential as the basis for an animation effect when it's extended over a series of frames. For example, you can reposition each letter with the Node Tool, creating animated bouncing text.

o n e
B u c   **B⁰ᵘⁿᵉ B u c**   **B⁰uⁿcᵉ**   **B⁰uⁿcᵉ**

Bounce   **B⁰uⁿcᵉ**   **B⁰uⁿcᵉ**   **B u c**

You can also...

- Vary the extent of transparency over text from frame to frame, producing a soft-edge wipe transition.

- Rotate text around its centre, corners or edge midpoints through 360°, while varying its size.

- Create a "flip" effect by vertically stretching and compressing text with respect to a central axis.

- Reduce or enlarge a text object as it moves toward a vanishing point.

- Employ curved text sequences that change over time.

Frame-edge effects

Suppose you want a collection of "bubbles" to appear to float out of a frame. The trick is to use the edge of the page (where it meets the pasteboard) as your frame, since any objects that extend beyond the page will be cropped when the animation is exported (although you'll still see them in the preview).

1. Set the page size to the correct proportions.

2. Since white space that's not used in any frame will be cropped out of the exported image, make sure at least one of the bubble objects touches each page edge at some point. This will preserve the frame proportions you've set (see left, below.)

3. To make bubbles appear to float out of the top of the frame, simply move them so they overlap the upper page edge. The result, when cropped on export, will be as shown on the right.

You can use a similar technique to bring objects in or out of the frame in any direction. The object makes a more convincing entrance (or exit) if it's shown as a partial object at the point of transition in (or out) of the frame.

Perception effects

Grab a book on optical illusions, or explore the Web for perception demonstrations. Sometimes quite eye-catching effects are possible with very simple combinations of lines and shapes.

- The **Whirlpool** Illusion: A Quick Spiral, available as a preset QuickShape, can be modified frame by frame resulting in a swirling effect—useful when drawing washing machines, a moving propeller, or even plug holes.

- The **Barber Pole** Illusion: A variation on the above, using diagonal stripes moving up or down, creates the effect of a rotating pole. Try using more of an S-shape to suggest a convex pole. Turned sideways, it becomes a twisting screw or worm gear.

Character animation

Character animation is beyond the scope of this chapter. But by using supplied samples, clipart and applying the basic principles, you can get amusing and effective results. For example, a cartoon cat can be simply drawn to create a "walking" motion frame by frame:

Remember to apply the concepts of stretching and squashing, overlapping frames for smooth movement, arc motion, and timing. Here are some other tips to keep in mind:

- **Anticipation**: You can set up a major action with a minor "get ready, get set" action. For example, before a frog leaps up into the air, it could squat down a bit. Subtle preparatory gestures like this add interest without adding a lot of extra frames.

- **Exaggeration**: In cartoons, virtually anything goes. Wild facial expressions, elastic arm and hand movements, and so on—just as long as the basic timing works.

- **Simplification**: Don't overdraw—take your cue from established cartoon conventions. There's probably a good reason why our favourite cartoon animals all seem to have only three fingers and a thumb!

Simulations

Realistic animations have a definite place in presentations and instructional materials. Whether you're demonstrating the beating of a heart, cog wheels turning, changes in a stock price, a route to follow on a map, or principles of basic physics, you can combine animated GIFs with HTML-based pages to deliver your message effectively.

- Consider using bitmaps as background frames and animating over them.

- Rather than trying to show too much or make too many points in one animation, break complex processes down into separate GIFs so each stage is conveyed clearly.

- Except for essential labels, place explanatory text and titles outside the animation to conserve file size.

- Scale file sizes to the delivery platform.

Using Transform

There are two methods available to transform objects for better animation, i.e.

- Transform tab. This is ideal for making precise positioning, resizing, rotational and shearing changes on your selected objects. Jump between the Frames and Transform tab to clone and transform for each frame sequence. The key feature is that the transform can be applied to an object's centre, any corner or any edge's midpoint.
  OR

- **Transform** dialog (available from **Transform...** on the Tools menu). This is ideal for generating sequences where an object appears to rotate or move from its centre. It lets you duplicate an object while applying a transform like rotation and/or offset with scaling. Its key feature is that the dialog allows multiple copies to be made and "remembers" the last transform you applied, so you can quickly repeat the effect over a series of successive frames.

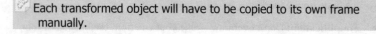 Each transformed object will have to be copied to its own frame manually.

Using Blends

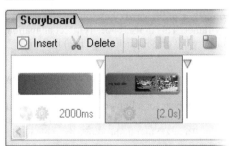 For stopframe animation of simple objects, you can make use of blending between objects to automatically create a stopframe for each blend step. After applying the blend, click the **Distribute Blend Objects onto Frames** button from the context toolbar. The Frames tab will be populated with each blended object, with your animation ready to run (although you can modify any object, add other objects, etc.).

You can perform this operation in Drawing mode (then **Convert to Stopframe Animation**) or from scratch in Stopframe Animation mode.

Working with Keyframe animation

When compared with Stopframe animation (see **Getting started with animation** on p. 174), **Keyframe animation** offers a more powerful and efficient animation technology—it's a valuable time-saver as it saves having to declare every frame, letting your computer do the hard work! Essentially, the technique lets you create only user-defined **keyframes**); through which objects animate, with each keyframe containing **Key objects**); which can be assigned a position, rotation, attributes, etc. Intermediate steps between Key objects are created automatically and produce a smooth professional-looking inter-object transition (this is called **Tweening**); Tweened objects are created as a result. You won't see these intermediate steps showing tweened objects by default, but they exist transparently between key objects throughout your animation.

The **Storyboard tab**, as its name suggests, is the workspace for laying out your animation "story" in a chronological keyframe-by-keyframe sequence (from left to right). On export, your animation will play in this direction.

Other tabs supporting the Storyboard tab are exclusively used within Keyframe animation, i.e.

- The **Easing tab** is used for applying linear or non-linear changes between key objects with use of editable envelopes (e.g., to change object position, morph, scale, rotation, skew, colour, and transparency).

- The **Actions tab** allows objects and keyframes to be attributed actions which will run (e.g., go to a URL or designated marker) when an event is triggered (e.g., MouseOver, Rollovers, etc.).

> 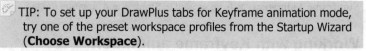 TIP: To set up your DrawPlus tabs for Keyframe animation mode, try one of the preset workspace profiles from the Startup Wizard (**Choose Workspace**).

DrawPlus takes a simple approach to building up your animation. By using a simple keyframe sequence of a bee, sun and some fun text you can understand the mechanics of the animation process. Only the bee is animated, the sun and "Buzzzz" text will be static objects.

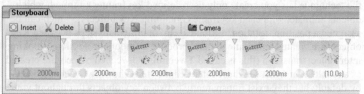

By adding objects (bee and sun) to a starting keyframe it's possible to automatically copy (or more correctly **run forward**) those objects forward when you create subsequent keyframes. This in itself doesn't affect animation, but it's the repositioning of a run forward object (such as the bee) in later keyframes that creates "movement".

Once keyframes are created, the animator has a great deal of control over how objects are run forward (or even backwards). You can introduce objects anywhere on the storyboard (so they appear for a limited time), and either run them forward or backwards by a specific number of keyframes (or right to the start or end of the storyboard). The "Buzzzz" text in the above example will only show during the combined duration of keyframes 3, 4, and 5 (i.e., 6 seconds).

> 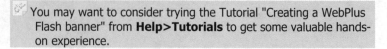 You may want to consider trying the Tutorial "Creating a WebPlus Flash banner" from **Help>Tutorials** to get some valuable hands-on experience.

For more advanced keyframe animation, DrawPlus provides a range of features for the more experienced user, i.e.

- Apply **actions** in response to object events or at a specific keyframe either via an easy-to-use dialog or develop ActionScript™ code directly.

- Use the **Keyframe camera** for panning, zooming and rotation effects over keyframes.

- **Masking** lets you produce cutaways, i.e. punching through a layer(s) to reveal underlying objects.

- Add **sound** and **movies** to enhance your animation.

Getting started

TIP: You can enter Keyframe animation mode via **File>New>New Keyframe Animation** or by converting your existing drawing by using **File>Convert to Keyframe Animation**.

Basic keyframe animations are created in a specific order:

1. Select a **Page Setup** from the context toolbar specific to your keyframe animation.

2. Create object(s), either static or for animation, on the page.

3. From the Storyboard tab, insert the number of keyframes and their duration via a dialog.

4. **Reposition** objects in subsequent keyframes to effect animation.

5. Export your keyframe animation as Adobe® Flash® (SWF).

Choosing a Page Setup:

1. Choose **Page Setup** from the context toolbar (shown with Pointer or Rotate Tool selected).

2. Either:

   - For a **custom** document size, enter a **Width** and **Height** (in pixels) and set the orientation (**Tall** for portrait, **Wide** for Landscape). Ensure the Custom is set from the **Size** drop-down menu.
   OR

- For **commonly used** document sizes, select from the **Size** drop-down menu.

    Any document size can be changed for another via the supporting context toolbar.

> TIP: Make use of the Startup Wizard's **Create>Keyframe Animation** or **Open>Design Template** options to choose preset page setups or animation templates, respectively.

To view the Storyboard tab:

- Unless the tab is already displayed, click the ▬▬▲▬▬ handle at the bottom of your workspace to reveal the tab.

We'll assume that you've drawn objects on the first keyframe. You can run forward these automatically throughout you animation by creation of additional keyframes—this builds up your animation "story" quickly. Other methods exist to run objects forward (and backwards) but let's concentrate on the insertion of keyframes to do this.

To insert keyframes:

1. From the Storyboard tab, select a keyframe and choose ⬚ Insert .

2. From the dialog, choose the **Number of keyframes** to add to the Storyboard tab. Set a default **Keyframe duration** for each created keyframe.

3. Choose to add keyframe(s) at a **Location** before or after the currently selected keyframe or before/after the first or last keyframe.

4. (Optional) Check **Insert blank keyframes** if you don't want to include run forward objects in your keyframes. Blank frames are useful "filler" frames that add breaks in your animation for messages, logos, etc.

5. Click **OK**.

An inserted frame will honour any animation runs that may transect it if the **Insert blank keyframes** setting remains unchecked (by creating an additional tweened object). If checked, the blank frame will break any transecting animation path(s) and not add tweened objects.

Once you've created a keyframe sequence you can sub-divide or split any selected keyframe further.

To split a selected keyframe:

1. Click the **Split keyframe** button on the Storyboard tab.

2. From the dialog, enter the number of divisions that the keyframe is to be split into, then click **OK**. Each new keyframe's duration is an equal division of the original keyframe's duration.

To view or edit a particular keyframe:

- Select a keyframe in the Storyboard tab.
  OR

- Click an object in an animation run that you know is associated with a specific keyframe (the keyframe will then be selected).

> TIP: Use your keyboard's **Page Up** and **Page Down** keys to navigate along your animation storyboard.

To delete a keyframe:

- Select the keyframe and choose **Delete**.

Keyframe duration

A keyframe's duration represents the amount of time the keyframe (and its objects) will be shown during animation playback. The value is set according to how the keyframe was created, i.e.

- Inserting keyframes (blank or otherwise) lets you set the keyframe duration in an Insert Keyframes dialog (default 1 second).

- A splitting operation will create new keyframes whose duration will be a division of the selected keyframe's duration (by the number of keyframes to be split).

A keyframe's duration can be altered manually at any time.

To set the duration of an individual keyframe:

- Click the keyframe's duration (e.g., 1000ms) under its thumbnail, and, when selected, type a new value then click away.

TIP: The total duration of your animation is shown on your last
keyframe, e.g. (5.0s).

Storyboard control

Storyboard control is possible by using a selection of buttons grouped
together on the Storyboard tab (equivalent options are on the Storyboard
menu). They operate across the entire storyboard, as opposed to on an
individual keyframe or key object.

Break storyboard	Breaks the animation run that transects through a selected keyframe into two separate runs.
Compact storyboard	A tool for tidying up your storyboard; any keyframes containing only tweened objects are removed from the storyboard.
Scale storyboard	Expands or shrinks the whole storyboard. All keyframe durations are automatically adjusted to fit proportionately to the new **Scale** duration.

Previewing keyframe animations

You can **preview** your animation at any time either in a web browser or in
Flash Player (installed during DrawPlus install). This is a quick way of
checking it prior to export.

To preview:

- Click the [button] button on the Storyboard tab, then from the drop-down
  menu choose to either:

  - **Preview in Browser....** The option displays a dialog which lets you
    preview in your web browser either standalone or by loading a target
    HTML page and associated SWF file (the target SWF file, e.g. a
    WebPlus banner, will be replaced by the animation to be previewed).
    Check **Preview using existing HTML file** for the latter, then
    navigate to and select HTML and SWF files.
    OR

- **Preview in Flash Player** (default). Use the navigation controls to review your animation as it would appear as an exported Flash SWF file. The animation loads Flash Player (if installed) and begins playing in a Flash Preview window.

If you chose not to install Flash Player during program install, you'll need to modify your install in Windows **Add or Remove Programs** (Start menu>Control Panel). Select the **Change** button, then choose the **Modify** button from the wizard, then enable the Flash Player option as part of the optional installs.

Keyframe object control

We've just looked at storyboard control. However, a whole series of important **object control** tools are also available in keyframe animation. They are available on an object toolbar, displayed in-context under any selected object.

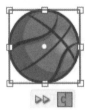

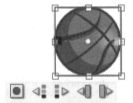

Initial grouped objects show run forward and grouped object buttons

Objects along the animation run show buttons for conversion to key objects, and object placement and attributes buttons in both directions.

The insertion of keyframes when you begin your animation will automatically run objects forward or backward. However, **Run Forward** and **Run Backward** commands let you introduce new objects in your animation which run across a limited number of keyframes or the entire storyboard.

To run object(s) forward/backward:

1. Select the keyframe which contains your chosen object.

2. Select the object, then click ▷▷ **Run forward** (or ◁◁ **Run backward** if on a later keyframe), located on the object toolbar directly under the selected object.

3. From the dialog, choose to **Run Length** either **To end of storyboard** or by **N Keyframes** (enter a number of keyframes to copy to). You can optionally run objects to the start of the storyboard or by a set number of previous keyframes.

Once run forward or backward, you can move an object on any keyframe (normally the last) to make animation work. Objects that are not moved are called **tweened objects**, and show as transparent square nodes (see below) which are automatically created between any two **key objects**. If you move any of these interim tweened objects you change your animation to follow a non-linear path (see below)—as a result, the tweened object becomes a key object.

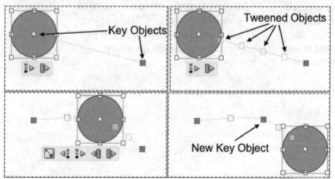

This takes care of repositioning objects, but what about changing an object's transform (morph, scale, rotation, and shear) or attribute (colour or transparency)? Simply, a selected tweened object can be modified just like any other object—it will be converted to a key object automatically as a transform or attribute change is applied.

> TIP: 🔘 🔳 Use **Convert to key object** to lock a tweened object into place (by making it a key object). Use the opposite command, **Convert to tweened object**, to convert back to a tweened object (removing any repositioning, transforms, or attributes local to the object). Both options are on the object toolbar.

The Object toolbar also offers two commands for repositioning objects along the storyboard. **Update placement backward** updates a previous object's position to match the selected key or tweened object's current position. Conversely, **Update placement forward** updates later object's position accordingly.

To change object placement:

1. Select the object whose positional information you want to apply forward or backward.

2. From the object's toolbar, click either:

    - ◀ **Update placement backward** to make a previous object's position match the selected object's position.
      OR

    - ▶ **Update placement forward** to do the same to later object positions.

3. From the dialog, choose to **Run Length** either to the beginning/end of the storyboard, or to a set number of keyframes before/after the currently selected object (choose the Run length drop-down menu, pick **N Keyframes** and enter a number of keyframes).

4. Click **OK**.

Like DrawPlus's **Format Painter**, you can also apply a specific object's attributes (colour, transparency, filter effects, shadows, etc.) to previous or later objects.

To change object attributes

1. Select the object whose attributes you want to apply forward or backward.

2. From the object's toolbar, click either:

   - The ◀▮ **Update attributes backward** button to apply attributes to previous objects.
   OR

   - The ▮▷ **Update attributes forward** button to apply attributes to later objects.

3. From the dialog, choose to **Run Length** either to the beginning/end of the storyboard, or to objects a set number of keyframes before/after the currently selected object (choose the Run length drop-down menu, pick **N Keyframes** and enter a number of keyframes to copy to).

4. Click **OK**.

You'll also find some useful options on the Run menu which can also be used to manipulate objects between keyframes or along the whole animation run.

Slide Forward/Backward	Moves a selected object forward/backward by a number of keyframes or to the end of the storyboard.
Repeat Forward/Backward	Extends the object forward/backward by a number of keyframes or to the end of the storyboard. Any animation run is extended as a result.
Delete All	Removes a selected object from the entire animation run in **both** directions.
Delete Forward/Backward	Removes a selected object from all previous or subsequent keyframes. Great for directional bulk removal throughout an animation run.
Duplicate	Creates a copy of the object directly on top of the existing object.
Reverse	Swaps the order of the objects along the animation run.

Some other settings affect how objects animate along the animation run. These are hosted on the Easing tab and control object rotation, temporal tweening, natural motion, and how keyframes obey a **Keyframe camera**. The settings are applied between key object "segments" (and will apply until the next key object) or throughout the animation's run depending on the **Apply to Whole Run** check box setting (unchecked or checked, respectively). When the option is unchecked, objects can adopt different combinations of settings independently of each other, i.e.

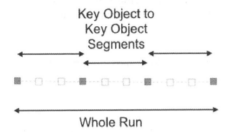

To configure a "segment", select the first Key object (■) then configure settings in the Easing tab (with Apply to Whole Run unchecked).

Clockwise Rotation	When checked, any rotation between objects is performed clockwise. Uncheck to rotate in an counter-clockwise direction.
Temporal Tween	Check to tween evenly between keyframes or over the whole storyboard (ignoring individual keyframe's time durations). Uncheck to honour any keyframe time durations. This is kept checked in most instances.
Natural Motion	When checked, animation occurs along a smoothed curving path through objects. Uncheck to animate along straight paths, with distinct corners at objects.
Rotate on path	Check to allow an object (e.g., an arrow) to automatically rotate with changes of direction along an animation path. Uncheck for the object to follow the path but not to re-align to it.
Obey camera	If using the **Keyframe camera** feature, when the option is checked then a selected object will be panned or zoomed into. When unchecked, the object remains static, ignoring the camera. Use when text (company logo, a message, etc.) is to be permanently presented while panning and zooming is performed in the background.

Autorun

Although switched off by default, this advanced feature speeds up the animation process by automatically creating objects, their placement and attributes along the length of the storyboard, from a specific keyframe onwards. Even when editing an object, the changes are reflected throughout. Without Autorun enabled, objects are presented across keyframes by using the Insert button or clicking the object toolbar's **Run forward** or **Run backward** buttons.

> The Autorun feature does not "autorun" objects backwards but instead only runs objects forward.

To autorun objects:

1. Click the 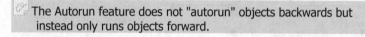 button on the Storyboard tab. The button is highlighted when enabled. Click again to disable.

2. Create or modify an object on a keyframe to see the effect on the object in subsequent keyframes.

As well as switching the Autorun feature on and off, you can also check one of the following options (click the down arrow on the Autorun button):

Creation and Placement	By default, an object will be created on every subsequent keyframe and object placement is mirrored throughout the subsequent keyframes of your storyboard.
Creation	The object is created on every subsequent keyframe throughout your storyboard but the object's position on keyframes remains unaffected.
Placement	The object's position is mirrored on subsequent keyframes on your storyboard.
Attributes	The attributes (colour, transparency, effects) of an object are mirrored to the same object on subsequent keyframes on your storyboard.

Applying actions (keyframe animation)

Selected objects can be assigned an event and corresponding **action**. The use of actions provides an interactive experience in response to a user's mouse up/down/press/release, key press/up/down, roll over, etc. As a typical example, an event such as a mouse press on an object can initiate an action such as a jump to a particular keyframe, e.g. an important point in your animation that could indicate contact details, important messages, etc.

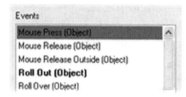

The **Actions tab** is used to apply actions to a selected object. By firstly selecting an event from the tab's Events scrolling list, you can then link that event to an available action—listed for selection within a single dialog, i.e.

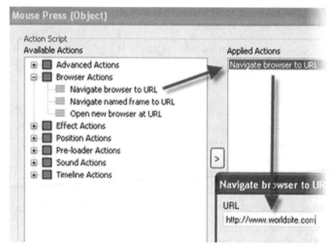

Actions are grouped into a tree menu structure whose categories include:

- **Advanced** Actions: Begin/End blocks, apply conditions, create variables, variable control.

- **Browser** Actions: navigate browser to URL (shown), navigate frame to URL Open browser with URL.

- **Effect** Actions: named object control (hide, show, recolour).

- **Position** Actions: move objects by pixel or to screen areas.

- **Pre-loader** Actions: rewind animation, object stretch.

- **Sound** Actions: increase/decrease volume, play/stop sound, set volume.

- **Timeline** Actions: go to marker, animation frame, animation playback control (stop, play, rewind).

When an action is applied from the menu you may be prompted for a parameter setting (pixel width, colour, etc) but you can alter parameters at any time—without having to view underlying ActionScript code.

Optionally, a new action can be created from scratch within the dialog. Simply code directly or paste ActionScript into a Edit window.

DrawPlus makes use of ActionScript, a language specifically designed for Adobe Flash applications, to allow a high level of interactivity between the exported Flash SWF and the user (e.g., a web visitor).

To apply an action to selected object(s):

1. Select an object on any keyframe.

2. Double-click an event from the Actions tab.

3. From the dialog, navigate the tree menu, expanding the options if necessary, and click on a chosen action (e.g., Timeline Actions>Goto marker X).

4. Click the ⊳ button to apply the selected action (it moves across into the Applied Actions box), then repeat for optional additional actions. You may be presented with a dialog which prompts for object names or parameter values (colours, number of pixels, marker names, etc.) required for the underlying ActionScript code to act on.

5. (Optional) For multiple applied actions, you can order the Applied Actions list with the **Up** or **Down** buttons.

6. Click **OK**. You'll notice the selected event now shown in bold (see **Roll Out (Object)** above) in the Actions tab.

The applied action can be edited by double-clicking the tab's bold event entry and, from the dialog, clicking the **Params** button (with object selected). To delete an action, use the **Delete** button to remove it.

We've looked at actions assigned to objects, but a keyframe can equally have an action associated with it. Especially useful on a starting keyframe, an Effect Action can be used to hide one or more selected objects before having them displayed on the second and subsequent keyframe (great for text introductions!). Actions are applied to keyframes via the **Frame Actions** dialog, which offers the same actions as those that can be applied to objects.

To apply action(s) to a keyframe:

• Right-click the chosen keyframe in the Storyboard tab and select **Frame Actions**.

The dialog displayed is identical to that used for actions applied to objects. Follow the above object actions procedure to apply actions to keyframes.

ActionScript, the underlying scripting language for actions, is normally hidden from the user in the above easy-to-use dialogs—you can view actions, their settings (as parameters), and select the action but generally not the underlying code driving it. However, the more experienced and/or adventurous can make use of a simple text entry system for developing ActionScript code from the same dialog.

To create custom ActionScript:

1. For a selected object, double-click an event from the Actions tab.
    OR
    For a keyframe, right-click the keyframe and choose **Frame Actions**.

2. Click the **New** button to add a New Action entry to the Applied Actions list.

3. With the entry selected, click the **Edit** button. The Action Script Code Editor window is displayed.

4. Enter your ActionScript code either by coding directly or by pasting existing code in the window.

5. Click **OK**.

Click the **Flatten** button to rationalize several listed actions into one. A combined action named "Flattened Code" is created instead. Each code snippet will be run consecutively.

ActionScript Version 2 is supported in DrawPlus.

Creating markers

▽ Working in a similar manner to bookmarks, markers work along with actions, allowing jumps to particular keyframes on the storyboard. Markers are positioned between keyframes along the storyboard and need to be activated for use. Each marker can be named, which is especially useful for marker identification when you're using multiple markers along your storyboard.

Additionally, a marker can be used to stop an animation, preventing your animation from looping—the **Stops playhead** marker setting will prevent the animation from continuing past that marker position.

To set a marker:

1. Click a ▽ marker icon after a chosen keyframe.

2. From the dialog, enter an easily identifiable **Marker Name**.

3. (Optional) Check **Stops playhead** to prevent your animation from continuing.

4. Click **OK**.

5. The marker's appearance will change accordingly, i.e.

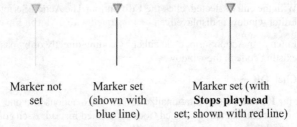

Marker not set | Marker set (shown with blue line) | Marker set (with **Stops playhead** set; shown with red line)

When used in conjunction with the Timeline Actions "Goto marker X" or "Goto marker X and stop" the exported animation can jump to different section according to a chosen object's event or the display of a keyframe.

Affecting change over time (keyframe animation)

DrawPlus uses the term **envelopes** to describe editable motion paths (or profiles) intended to define the rate of change (acceleration/deceleration) to an object's transformation or physical attributes (colour or transparency) in your animation run.

Envelopes are applied, created, modified and saved in the **Easing tab**. A series of envelope types can be applied between key objects in your animation or throughout the entire animation run. Typically, a non-linear **Position envelope** would alter how an object speeds up or slows down over the animation run. Other envelope types can alter the rate of transformation such as Rotate, Morph, Scale, and Skew.

You can manually edit any profile independently of each other such that you may have a mix of edited profiles and default linear ones. The Easing tab's **Envelope type** drop-down menu lets you select your envelope type, allowing you to then define a profile shape for that envelope in the pane. In most instances, an "All Envelopes" option can be used to affect a variable rate of change for **all** envelopes simultaneously.

The process or editing an envelope is identical, irrespective of envelope type. By default, any envelope is applied linearly (i.e., they change at a uniform rate over time) so you have to manually edit the envelope to apply a non-linear rate of change.

The differing rates of change of can be illustrated with a Morph Envelope between two simple QuickShapes.

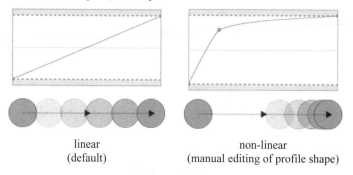

linear
(default)

non-linear
(manual editing of profile shape)

To apply an envelope:

1. Display the Easing tab.

2. Select an object from the Storyboard tab to which you want to apply the envelope.

3. Select a profile from the **Envelope type** drop-down menu (Easing tab). The displayed profile will be linear by default (see above), unless you've applied the envelope previously.

4. Hover over the turquoise line (the cursor changes to ⤳) and drag in any direction to position a newly created red node. Repeat the process for the number of nodes that you want to add to make up the profile. You can then fine-tune the profile shape by adjusting node positions accordingly.

> TIP: Edit an existing profile from the preset drop-down menu to create profiles quickly.

DrawPlus will keep the applied profile unless you modify it or you reset the profile manually. If you'll be using the profile shape in the future you can save the current settings to your own saved profile.

To reset an envelope:

1. Select the correct envelope from the **Envelope Type** drop-down menu (Easing tab).

2. Click the ⊗ Reset button.

To create a new preset:

1. Modify the profile shape from an existing preset (or create from scratch).

2. Select **Add Easing Profile** from the Easing tab's ▷ **Tab Menu** button to save it. The new profile will appear at the bottom of the **Envelope Profiles** drop-down menu.

To delete a profile preset:

1. Select **Manage Easing Profiles...** from the ▷ **Tab Menu**.

2. From the dialog, select the preset entry, then click the **Delete** button.

Keyframe animation tips and tricks

So far the emphasis has been on creating simple animations from scratch, keyframe/object control, and how change over time is affected.

In order to go one step further, and create more complex animations, you may want to explore more advanced features ranging from using Keyframe camera effects, applying masking effects, and changing an object's state.

Using the Keyframe camera

The camera effect lets you pan, zoom or rotate areas of your animation to create a more interesting visual appeal. Especially useful if you want to focus on parts of your animation (e.g., a main cartoon character or a company logo, telephone number, or web address), the feature is very powerful and should be used without making too many dramatic transformations (try zooming by small amounts over the animation duration).

To enable the Keyframe camera:

1. Select a keyframe to which you want to apply a pan, zoom or rotate operation.

2. To enable, click the ⟨⟨⟩⟩ Camera button on the Storyboard tab. A single rectangular bounding box (shown with a solid blue border) is shown around the page which defines the visible area to be displayed. You'll notice a camera appear as a layer entry under the current layer in the Layers tab.

3. Reposition and/or resize the bounding box to set an initial view level that the animation can display.

4. (Optional) Set the bounding box in other keyframes, according to the desired effect. Otherwise a full screen view will be used in the remaining keyframes.

> TIP: With the camera enabled, select 📷 **Reset Keyframe Camera** on the object's toolbar to revert the display area back to the default.

For specific objects that are to ignore pan, zoom and rotation (think of a company logo which needs to remain static throughout the animation), with the object selected, uncheck **Obey Camera** on the Easing tab.

Masking

The option lets you mask one or more layers immediately below a purposely created mask layer. Mask layer objects cut away to reveal only underlying layer's objects showing under the mask object (the remainder is masked from view)—great for creating circular spotlights, keyhole shapes, or any other conceivable object shape. QuickShapes are ideal for this but don't discount using Artistic Text for interesting cutouts.

Try experimenting with a stationary mask layer with animation being performed on lower layers, animation on both mask and non-mask layers, or you could just animate the mask itself.

To create a mask:

1. With the Layers tab displayed, create a layer intended purposely for masking object(s), then place it directly **above** the layer(s) you want to mask.

2. Draw one or more objects on this mask layer. You can overlap objects but you won't need to combine the objects or worry about object fills (DrawPlus will work it out!). However, you might like to group multiple objects together.

3. (Optional) To mask multiple layers, double-click the mask layer and set the number of **layers** in the dialog's Attributes box.

4. (Optional) Run your selected mask objects forward and reposition them either at the end of the animation run or on a selected prior keyframe. This will allow the masked objects to animate.

5. Click the ▣ **Mask** button on the new mask layer (it then shows as Ⓜ).

6. To enable masking, click the adjacent 🔒 **Locked** button (this also locks the mask objects in place).

State behaviour

By default, any object drawn in DrawPlus is considered to be a **non-state object** (i.e., one that has a single set of attributes). Within Keyframe animation it's possible to convert such a non-state object to a **state object** by assigning it one or more "states" such as Normal, Hover, or Pressed, with each state possessing its own object attributes.

The advantage here is that in each state, the object can have a different appearance in response to a user event such as a mouse press or mouse hover over. This lets you creates interactive intelligent objects which change with your mouse movement/actions. Think of a "Play" button on your computer's music/video player having different appearance when clicked.

In DrawPlus, an object's state is indicated by its adjacent state buttons shown next to the object (only two states will be shown at any time; the third state is the current object's state).

For example, an object in Normal state shows adjacent 🔲 **Hover** and 🔲 **Pressed** buttons, i.e.

If you click either button you'll jump to that state's sub-object. If in Hover or Pressed state, you'll see the 🔲 **Normal** button.

To convert to a state object:

1. Select the object.

2. Choose **State>Convert to state object** from the Object menu.

Use the **Convert to non-state object** from the same menu if you want convert back.

To change an object's attributes:

- Click the state buttons to toggle between the different modes.

- Once in a chosen mode, modify the sub-object attributes (colour, transparency, effects, etc.) that will show for that mode (i.e., as **Normal**, on mouse **Hover**, or when the mouse is **Pressed**).

The use of state behaviours does not prevent you from assigning your own Actions to the different sub-objects. In fact, it's likely that you may want to show an object (e.g., a button) change colour on hover over, then jump to a URL on a subsequent mouse press.

Exporting animations

Exporting your stopframe or keyframe animation outputs your animation to a file which can be shared or viewed, either standalone or when included as part of a web page. DrawPlus lets you export to a variety of formats as indicated below:

Export	Stopframe	Keyframe
Flash SWF	✗	✓
Video	✓	✓
Image	✓	✓
CAD/CAM	✓	✗
Screensaver	✗	✓
Flash Lite/i-Mode	✗	✓

Flash SWF

The **Flash SWF** (ShockWave Flash) format has fast become the format of choice for interactive vector-based graphic animation for the Web. Great for creating a simple or sophisticated animated toolbar for Web Page navigation, it is universally supported on Web browsers. The files can be easily manipulated further (scaled, etc.) within Adobe® Flash®.

To export your animation as a Flash file:

1. Choose Export>Export as Flash SWF... from the File menu.

2. From the dialog, provide a ShockWave Flash file name and folder location, and click the **Save** button. You'll see an export progress dialog appear until the Flash file is created.

Video

Exported **video** formats include:

- **QuickTime**. The QuickTime video and animation format (**MOV**) developed by Apple Computer. It can be read on many platforms, including Microsoft Windows (needs QuickTime plug-in) and of course on Apple computers. QuickTime supports most encoding formats, including Cinepak, JPEG, and MPEG.

- **Serif Transparent Video**. The STV format is a useful proprietary format which can export animated text and logos with transparent backgrounds. The export benefits Serif MoviePlus users who would like to use their keyframe animation as an overlay (of titles, animated characters, etc.).

- **Video for Windows**. The Windows Audio Video Interleave file (**AVI**) is ideal for playback on a Windows computer. Defined by Microsoft, it supports different types of video, audio and image sequences in sync with a mono or stereo sound track along with compression (via a wide variety of codecs). AVIs are mainly for viewing on a computer. Appropriate codecs have to be installed on the computer.

- **Windows Media audio and Video**. The **WMV** format is best supported on PCs running Windows Media Player, although some other software even on other platforms can play WMV video. WMVs are Advanced Systems Format (.ASF) files that include audio, video, or both compressed with Windows Media Audio (WMA) and Windows Media Video (WMV) codecs.

- The **.GIF**. format is ideal for Web as it's universally supported by Web browsers, and, as it's a multi-part format, it's capable of encoding not just one image but multiple images in the same file. A .GIF animation player or Web browser can display these images in sequence, in accordance with certain settings (looping, frame delay, etc.) included in the file. The result—it moves! As with single-frame GIFs, if you opt to export your animation with the Transparency setting turned on, any unfilled regions of the graphic will become transparent in the GIF. All other regions will become opaque. Keyframe animation cannot export Animated GIFs. For details on using transparency in GIFs, see **Using transparency effects** on p. 165.

To export animation as video:

1. Choose **Export>Export As Video...** from the File menu.

2. From the displayed dialog's Basic tab, select your chosen export type from the **File type** and **Template** drop-down list according to the type of output video format you require.

3. (Optional) Click **Match project settings** to set an approximate video frame size based on your animation project's Page size (set in Page Setup).

4. Specify a name for file in the **Filename** box, clicking **Browse** and selecting a new location if you first wish to choose an alternate drive or folder to store your file.

5. (Optional) From the dialog's Advanced tab, make a new video template with the **Copy** button, then alter more advanced settings such as video Frame size (choose Custom then set a Width and Height), Pixel aspect ratio, Frame rate, Interlacing, Codec settings, and more, depending on the format to be exported. (See Exporting video (Advanced) in DrawPlus help for more details).

6. (Optional) Set an export **Quality**.

7. Click the **Export** button. Your project will then be composed and converted into the specified format and you will be shown a progress bar during this process.

Image

Within Stopframe animation, this option lets you create an animated GIF by default, which we'll focus on here. For keyframe animation, you can export a single keyframe as any type of image format. However, it's also possible to export any Stopframe as an image, but this is covered elsewhere in **Exporting object and drawings** (see p. 241).

To export as an animated GIF:

1. Choose [Export] from the Frames tab. The Export Optimizer appears.

2. In the **Format** tab, the Animated GIF format is pre-selected on the **Format** drop-down menu by default; if not, select it. If you choose another format, only the current frame will be exported. For full details on GIF export options, consult **Exporting objects and drawings**.

3. From the **Settings tab**, set a size for the GIF animation and whether it is based on the whole page, selected regions or objects. Leave the dpi setting at 96 for standard screen resolution.

4. On the **Animation tab**, which only appears in Stopframe Animation Mode, you can preview single frames or run the animation sequence, and make some final playback adjustments to the animation properties.

5. Click the **Export** button (or **Close** to simply record the settings if you plan to preview in a browser first).

6. Provide a file name and folder location, and click **Save**. Don't worry if you have extra white space around your image. Any unused border area will be cropped automatically, just as you saw in the Preview window.

Screensaver

If you're working with keyframe animations, you also have the option of creating a screensaver file (.SCR). Your Windows-compatible exported file can be used on your computer (as for any screensaver file) or for distribution to friends and family equally.

To create a screensaver:

1. Choose Export>Export as Screensaver... from the File menu.

2. From the **Save As** dialog, enter a screensaver file name and folder location. Remember to save your file into the following locations for the screensaver to be viewable and enabled in Windows 2000 or XP:

   - For Windows 2000: C:\WINNT\SYSTEM32\
     OR

   - For Windows XP: C:\WINDOWS\SYSTEM32\

3. In the next dialog provide a title and contents for your screensaver's About box, then click the **OK** button.

4. Click the **Save** button. You'll see an export progress dialog appear until the screensaver file is created.

To enable the Screensaver:

1. Right-click on your Windows Desktop background and select **Properties**.

2. From the dialog, select the **Screen Saver** tab.

3. Select your screensaver from the **Screen Saver** drop-down list.

4. (Optional) Use the **Wait** input box to set an idle duration before your screensaver will be displayed.

Flash Lite/i-Mode

Use if you're intending to export a keyframe animation for mobile users operating mobile phones, personal organizers, and more. The format is optimized for viewing on smaller screen displays. The outputted file type is the same as that for Flash export, with a SWF file extension.

To export to Flash Lite/i-Mode:

1. Choose Export>Export as Flash Lite/i-Mode... from the File menu.

2. From the dialog, provide a ShockWave Flash file name and folder location, and click the **Save** button. You'll see an export progress dialog appear until the file is created.

10
Importing

Importing pictures

DrawPlus lets you import pictures from a wide variety of file formats. Here's a quick overview:

- **Bitmapped** pictures, also known as **bitmaps** or **raster** images, are built from a matrix of dots ("pixels"), rather like the squares on a sheet of graph paper. They may originate as digital camera photos or scanned images, or be created (or enhanced) with a "paint" program or photo editor. When imported, it becomes the Bitmap fill for a new Quick Box object. As with other object fills, you can add these bitmaps to the Bitmap fill gallery to be used as fills for other objects. For details, see "**Changing the set of Bitmap gallery fills**" on p. 162.

- **Draw** graphics, also known as **vector** graphics are resolution-independent and contain drawing commands such as "draw a line from A to B." These are like DrawPlus drawings, made of many individual objects grouped together, and you can edit them in the same sort of way. You have the choice of ungrouping the objects in order to edit them further, or leaving them as a group. When imported, DrawPlus first converts it to a metafile and then converts the metafile into individual objects. You'll have the option of ungrouping the objects in order to edit them, or leaving them as a group.

- **Metafiles** are the native graphics format for Windows and combine raster and vector information.

Any imported picture ends up as an object you can select, move, scale, shear, rotate—and even crop using the Envelope Tool on the Drawing toolbar.

To import a picture from a file:

1. Click the **Insert Picture** button on the Drawing toolbar.

2. Use the Insert Picture dialog to browse files and select the file to import, then click **OK**. The dialog disappears and the mouse pointer changes to the Picture Size cursor. What you do next determines the initial size, placement, and aspect ratio (proportions) of the image.

3. Either:

- To insert the picture at a default size, simply click the mouse. OR

- To set the size of the inserted picture, drag out a region and release the mouse button.

Normally, the picture's aspect ratio is preserved. To allow free dragging to any aspect ratio, hold down the **Shift** key. To constrain the aspect ratio to a square, hold down the **Ctrl** key.

As another import technique, DrawPlus lets you use "autotracing" to import a bitmap as a vector graphic.

To import a bitmap as a vector graphic:

1. Choose **Picture>Autotrace...** from the Insert menu.

2. Use the file selection dialog to browse files and select the file to import, then click **OK**. An Autotrace dialog appears with the original image displayed on the left.

3. Click the **Trace** button to preview the autotraced image on the right.

4. To adjust the scale of the images, click the 🔍 **Zoom** button, then left-click in the preview region to zoom in or right-click to zoom out. To view specific regions, click the 🖑 **Pan** button, then drag.

5. Adjust the **Smoothness** setting (0-10) to adjust the degree of "median cut" (noise reduction) filtering, and/or **Tolerance** (0-255) to vary the degree of colour mixing, until you've achieved an optimal preview image. Click **Trace** after each adjustment to update the preview. The **Polygon count** box reports the complexity of the resulting vector image, which is directly related to file size.

6. When you're done, click **OK**, then click or drag to insert the picture.

Notes:

- You can **import camera and scanner images** via TWAIN Acquire (see p. 215).

- Once placed, you can swap the picture with the 🖼 Replace Picture button on the Picture context toolbar.

- You can always resize a picture as required, after it's been placed, by dragging its handles. For the finer points of resizing, see **Resizing objects** on p. 119.

- For image adjustment, a Picture context toolbar appears automatically when you select an image on the page. You can adjust **brightness**, **contrast**, **Red Eye** or apply **Auto Level** or **Auto Contrast**. To fix photo deficiencies, select the toolbar's **Image Adjustments** button. Image adjustments are made possible with a comprehensive mix of colour correction/adjustment tools for use on your newly imported images. **Levels**, **Colour Balance**, **Channel mixer**, **Dust and Scratch Remover** and **Hue/Saturation/Lightness** corrective adjustments, amongst others, are available for use individually or cumulatively. See DrawPlus help for further information.

Importing camera and scanner images

Photos from digital cameras and images created via scanner can be easily imported onto the DrawPlus page. In recent years, the increasingly more sophisticated image management software supplied with such digital devices means that DrawPlus leaves the photo management aspect of importing photos and images to the manufacturer's software (installed with the device on your computer). However, what DrawPlus will offer is the ability to choose between different TWAIN sources, launch the manufacturer's software automatically and subsequently place any chosen photos/images onto the DrawPlus page.

To set up your digital device for image acquisition:

- Follow the instructions supplied with the device.

When acquiring images from a camera that appears in Windows as a Removable Disk, ensure that you follow recommended procedures for connecting and disconnecting the device.

To import pictures from a digital camera or TWAIN device (scanner):

1. If you have multiple TWAIN-compatible devices, choose the device from which your image will be acquired—
    Picture>TWAIN>Select Source from the Insert menu lets you select your device from a menu.

2. For scanning or photo import, choose **Picture>TWAIN>Acquire** from the Insert menu to open the device's image management dialog. Follow the device manufacturer's instructions, and select the scanned image or photo for import.

3. In DrawPlus, the ▓ Picture Size cursor is displayed which allows image/photo to be placed at default size (by single-click) or sized (by dragging across the page).

> Colour scanned images can get very large and you need to take this into consideration. Large files take a long time to load, save and print; and they eat your disk space!

Importing other media

We've just looked at importing **pictures** or **scanned images** into your drawing or Stopframe animation. However, you can also import movie or audio clips exclusively into any Keyframe animation.

For Drawing mode or any Animation mode, media files already placed can be managed from one central location. DrawPlus makes this possible with the **Media tab** and allows viewing and direct replacement of media.

Adding sound

To complement the visual effect of your keyframe animation it's equally popular to add audio. Sounds can be added either for the duration of a specific keyframe, or when an action is applied to an object event (see **Applying actions** on p. 197 for details on actions and events).

To add an audio clip:

1. On the Storyboard tab, click on the keyframe's 🔊 **Sound** icon (located below the frame's thumbnail)

2. From the dialog, navigate to your audio file, select it and click the **Open** button.

To remove a selected keyframe's audio clip, right-click and select **Clear Background Sound**.

Adding movies

As well as using sound in your keyframe animation, you can introduce movie clips. The movie is inserted into your chosen keyframe as an object which like any other object (QuickShape, Text, etc.) will need to be run forward for the movie to play throughout the animation.

DrawPlus supports various video formats including Flash Video (FLV), Flash SWF, AVI, WMV, and QuickTime.

To add a movie:

1. Select the keyframe to which the movie is to be added.

2. Click the 📹 **Insert Movie Clip** button on the Drawing toolbar.

3. From the dialog, navigate to your movie file. Remembering to check that the correct **Files of type** drop-down menu option is set.

4. Select the movie file and click the **Open** button.

5. Position the displayed ⊹ cursor where you want the movie to appear.

6. Either:

    *   To insert the movie at the movie's original size, simply click the mouse.
        OR

    *   To set the size (and aspect ratio) of the inserted movie, drag out a region and release the mouse button.

7. (Optional) Use the object toolbars' controls to run forward/backward to the end/start of the storyboard (or by a set number of keyframes).

Using the Media tab

The **Media tab** displays already placed media in different categories: All Types, Bitmap Images (shown), Movie Clips, Audio Clips, or Text Fragments. To make things easy the default All Types category shows all media present in your drawing or animation. A media file will show its thumbnail for easy visual identification, its file name and dimensions (images), duration (movies) or actual text (text fragments).

For any media file, a double-click or right-click on the file will let you swap out the file for another (via a dialog). Alternatively right-click, then choose **Replace Media** (see opposite).

As already placed media is replaced by new media content you'll need to ensure attributes (image dimensions, movie run time, text length) are identical. Always check your new content visually and manipulate your media if necessary.

11

Special Effects

Creating text effects and logos

Besides drop shadows and related **2D filter effects**, DrawPlus features a variety of ways to enhance text in your drawings and animations. We'll mention a few here; the additional possibilities (for example, **fill effects, transparency effects, perspective effects, combination effects, 3D filter effects**, and **Instant 3D**) are endless!

Text in a shape. Using a shape and the Artistic Text Tool lets your **shape text** conform to the containing shape!

Text along a curve. Use the Curve Text Wizard or text context toolbar's Curve Text flyout to make artistic text conform to a curved baseline. For a special effect you will want the text to follow a regular path such as a circle, spiral, arc, or a drawn curve.

Enveloped text. Use the Envelope Tool or Envelope Wizard to distort artistic text to any outline shape.

To flow text in a shape:

- Select a shape (QuickShape or your own shape) and choose the Text Tool. Click within the bounding area of the shape and start typing.

To flow text along a curve:

Either:

1. If you want to use an existing text object, select the object first. Otherwise, you can enter text in the wizard.

2. Go to Tools>Curve Text Wizard.

3. After the first screen, enter text to be placed on the curve. This is not shown if text has already been selected on the page.

4. In the second screen, if an object or outline has already been selected the **Use Current Selection** option will be checked. Uncheck if you want your text to flow along one of the available preset curves then pick a curve on which the text will be placed.

5. Click **Finish** to close the wizard. This will display your text arranged on the curve, line or shape.

Or:

1. Select your artistic text.

2. From the context toolbar, click the button and select a preset curve from the drop-down menu on which the text will flow.

> Note: You can edit the baseline curve with the Node Tool.

To flow text into an envelope:

- (Using the Envelope Wizard) Choose **Envelope Wizard** from the Tools menu, follow the on-screen questions and enter your own information.
  OR

- (Using the Envelope Tool) Select one or more artistic text objects and click the **Envelope Tool** on the Drawing toolbar. Either drag the blue node handles to a new position to create a new envelope shape or choose **Preset Envelopes** from the Envelope context toolbar (see **Applying envelopes** on p. 71).

Creating borders

The **Border Wizard** lets you create a border around the whole page or a selected object, or within a specific page region. It's possible to create your own border from a current object selection or from a preset border style.

To create a border:

1. (If creating a border around an object) Select the object first.

2. Select **Border Wizard...** from the Insert menu.

3. From the dialog, choose to select a border from a library of pre-designed borders (From Library) or make your own border (based on the Current selection). Click **Next>**.

4. Choose which type of border you want (Whole page, Around the current selection, or Custom size and position) and click **Next**.

5. For presets, choose one of the pre-defined border designs from the scrolling list, and set the border's width. If making your own border, enable a different border style. The preview window shows what the border will look like in both instances.

6. Click **Finish**.

✥

If you chose a whole-page or object border, it appears immediately. With the "custom" option, use the cursor to drag out a region to be bordered.

Creating blends

Blends enable you to "morph" any shape into any other shape via the
Blend Tool. If the two shapes are separated in space, each step creates an
intermediate shape, to create a kind of morphing effect where the colour,
transparency and line properties all change along with the object shape during
the blend process.

The context toolbar shown when the Blend Tool is selected also lets you
adjust a number of blend settings before or after blending, i.e.

- the number of steps between the blend (to increase/decrease the
  smoothness of the blend)

- rate of transform via a set **Position Profile**

- rate of blend via **Attribute Profile**

- the Colour Blend Type

For more complex blending possibilities, objects can be multiply-blended
(to/from other blends) to create truly stunning illustrations. It is possible to
leap frog between separate shaped objects to create daisy-chained blends (by
click and drag on each object consecutively).

To create a blend with the Blend Tool:

1. Select the [image] **Blend Tool** button on the Drawing toolbar.

2. (Optional) From the displayed context toolbar, choose:

   - the number of "morph" **Blend Steps** to be taken between both points.

   - a Position or Attribute Profile for non-uniform blends. (See DrawPlus help).

   - a **Colour blend type** which defines how colour distribution occurs between the originating and destination object. You can **Fade** between colours by default, apply a **Clockwise/Anti Clockwise** colour spread around the HSL Colour Wheel (from Colour tab), or use the **Shortest** or **Longest** route between colours on the HSL Colour Wheel.

3. Hover over the object to display the Blend cursor.

4. Click and drag the cursor, drawing a dashed line as you go, to your destination point (this must be on an object) and release. Your blend is created. If blending to multiple objects, remember to group them in advance.

5. (Optional) Click the [image] **Convert Blend Object into a Group Object** button on the context toolbar to group all blended objects.

Any blend can be modified at a later date via the context toolbar.

Blends in Stopframe animation

For Stopframe animation of simple objects, you can make use of blending between objects to create frames automatically. You can perform this operation in Drawing mode (then **Convert to Stopframe Animation**) or from scratch in Stopframe Animation mode. See **Stopframe animation tips and tricks** on p. 180 for more information.

Creating rough edges

The **Roughen Tool** lets you selectively distort an object's outline, turning smooth-line edges into jagged outlines. The effect can lend cartoon-like flair to ordinary text or give QuickShapes an irregular appearance ...in fact apply it whenever it seems to suit the mood of the design.

To apply roughening:

1. Select an object and click the [image] **Roughen Tool** button on the Drawing toolbar.

2. Click on the object and drag up or down. The further you drag, the more pronounced the effect.

Applying shadows, glow, bevel, and emboss

DrawPlus provides a variety of **filter effects** that you can use to transform any object. The standard or 2D filter effects are especially well adapted to text, as shown here:

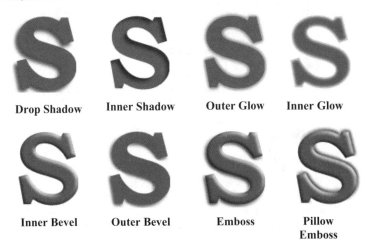

| Drop Shadow | Inner Shadow | Outer Glow | Inner Glow |

| Inner Bevel | Outer Bevel | Emboss | Pillow Emboss |

An object's 2D filter effect can be applied or edited singularly via a Filter Effects dialog, equipped with a branching checklist of available effects. Multiple effects can also be applied cumulatively.

To apply a shadow, glow, bevel, or emboss filter effect:

1. Select an object and choose **Filter Effects...** from the Format menu.

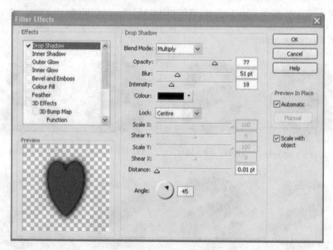

2. To apply one or more effects, check appropriate boxes in the list at left. Select an effect name to display the dialog specific to that effect.

3. For Shadow and Glow effects, choose a blend mode from the list. Click the **Colour** swatch to change the base highlight or shadow colour from its default (either white or black). Choose controls for shadow Scale and Shear (on X or Y axis).
    OR
    For Bevel and Emboss effects, choose a Highlight blend mode from the list and set the Opacity slider. Click the **Colour** swatch and change the highlight colour from its default (white). Then choose a Shadow blend mode, opacity, and colour (default black).

4. To adjust the properties of a specific effect select its name and vary the dialog controls. Adjust the sliders or enter specific values to vary the combined effect. (You can also select a slider and use the keyboard arrows.) Options differ from one effect to another.

5. Check the **Scale with object** box if you want the effect to adjust in proportion to any change in the object's size. With the box unchecked, the effect's extent remains fixed if you resize the object.

6. Click **OK** to apply the effect to the selected object, or **Cancel** to abandon changes.

Using the Shadow Tool

Shadows are great for adding flair and dimension to your work, with text objects or QuickShapes. To help you create shadows, you can use the **Shadow Tool** on the Drawing toolbar. This tool affords freeform control of the shadow effect and with its on-the-page control nodes and supporting Shadow context toolbar the tool offers various adjustments—Opacity, Blur, and X (or Y) Shear can be altered equally.

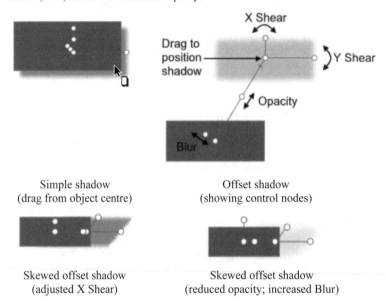

Simple shadow (drag from object centre)	Offset shadow (showing control nodes)
Skewed offset shadow (adjusted X Shear)	Skewed offset shadow (reduced opacity; increased Blur)

Once you've created a basic shadow, you can further edit it as needed using the Filter Effects dialog (see above).

To apply a shadow to selected object:

1. Click the [ ] **Shadow Tool** on the Drawing toolbar. You'll notice control nodes appear which allow adjustment as described in the illustration above.

2. Drag across the object to create a shadow (note additional nodes being created). Make any adjustments accordingly with nodes (or via the displayed context toolbar).

To change a shadow's colour:

- Choose the **Shadow Tool** and then select the object with the shadow applied. Select a colour from the Studio's Colour tab or pick a thumbnail from a solid colour palette in the Swatches tab. As long as the Shadow Tool is selected, colours are applied to the shadow, not to the object.

To remove the shadow from an object:

- Double-click the object while the Shadow Tool is selected.

> You can't edit an object's shadow with the Node Tool, or detach it from the object. As long as an object has a shadow property, its shadow will simply mirror any changes you make to the object itself.

Using 3D filter effects

3D filter effects go beyond 2D filter effects (shadows, bevel, emboss, etc.) to create the impression of a textured surface on the object itself. You can use the Filter Effects dialog to apply one or more effects to the same object—**3D Bump Map**, **2D Bump Map**, **3D Pattern Map**, **2D Pattern Map** and **3D Lighting**. Keep in mind is that none of these 3D effects will "do" anything to an unfilled object—you'll need to have a fill there to see the difference they make!

The Studio's **Effects tab** is a good place to begin experimenting with 3D filter effects. Its multiple categories each offer a gallery full of predefined effects, using various settings.

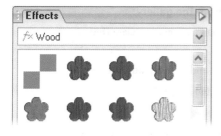

There you'll see a variety of remarkable 3D surface and texture presets in various categories (Glass, Metal, Wood, etc.). Click any thumbnail to apply it to the selected object. Assuming the object has some colour on it to start with, you'll see an instant result! Note that none of these effects will work on objects using the "Instant 3D" effect as described in the next section. Nor will they "do" anything to an unfilled object—you'll need to have a fill there to see the difference they make!

Alternatively, you can customize an Effects tab preset, or apply one or more specific effects from scratch, by choosing **Filter Effects...** from the Format menu. In the Filter Effects dialog, check the **3D Effects** and **3D Lighting** boxes (if customizing they will already be checked). The master settings of Blur and Depth make a great difference; you can click the "+" button to unlink them for independent adjustment. As for 3D Lighting, without a "light source" switched on, the depth information in the effect wouldn't be visible. You can also store an object's customized effect on the Studio's Effects tab to use later, as described below.

For more information about creating 3D filter effects, see DrawPlus help.

Customizing the set of gallery effects

Once you've customized an effect locally, you can add the effect into a gallery on the Effects tab so that it will be available to use again, and you can delete effects from the gallery. You can also add and delete your own gallery categories.

To add an object's effect to the gallery:

1. Display (or create, see below) the gallery category where you want to add the effect.

2. Right-click the object and choose **Add to Studio>Effect...** (or choose the item from the Format menu).

Once you've assigned a name to the effect, a thumbnail for it appears in the currently displayed gallery category.

To delete an existing effect from the gallery:

● Right-click the effect's thumbnail and choose **Delete Design....**

To create a gallery category:

1. Right-click in the category list and choose **Add Category....**

2. Type a name for the category and click **OK**.

To delete a gallery category:

● Right-click the category name and choose **Delete Category....**

Feathering

Feathering is a filter effect that adds a soft or blurry edge to any object. It's great for blending single objects into a composition, vignetted borders on photos, and much more. You can apply feathering in conjunction with other filter effects. (For details, see **Applying shadows, glow, bevel, and emboss** on p. 227 and **Using 3D filter effects** on p. 230.)

To apply feathering:

1. Select an object and choose **Filter Effects...** from the Format menu. The Filter Effects dialog appears.

2. Check the **Feather** box at left.

3. Adjust the sliders or enter specific values to vary the feathering effect. (You can also select a slider and use the keyboard arrows.)
   ● **Opacity** (0 to 100%) controls the opacity of shadow pixels.
   ● **Blur** controls the "fuzziness" of the edge.

4. Check the **Scale with object** box if you want the effect to adjust in proportion to any change in the object's size. With the box unchecked, the effect's extent remains fixed if you resize the object.

5. Click **OK**.

Applying dimensionality (Instant 3D)

Using the **Instant 3D** feature, you can easily transform flat shapes (shown) and text into three-dimensional objects.

DrawPlus provides control over 3D effect settings such as:

- **bevelling**: use several rounded and chiselled preset profiles or create your own.

- **lighting**: up to eight editable and separately coloured lights can be positioned to produce dramatic lighting effects.

- **lathe effects**: create contoured objects (e.g., a bottle cork) with user-defined lathe profiles and extrusion control.

- **texture**: control how texture is extruded on objects with non-solid fills.

- **viewing**: present your object in three dimensions.

- **material**: controls the extent to which lighting has an effect on the object's surfaces (great for 3D artistic text!).

An always-at-hand 3D context toolbar hosted above your workspace lets you configure the above settings—each setting contributes to the 3D effect applied to the selected object. For on-the-page object control you can transform in 3D with use of a blue orbit circle, which acts as an axis from which you can rotate around the X-, Y-, and Z-axes in relation to your page. Look for the cursor changing as you hover over either the circles' nodes or periphery.

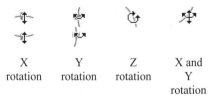

| X rotation | Y rotation | Z rotation | X and Y rotation |

Remember to take advantage of the hover-over cursor text or hintline which indicate the object's rotation currently or rotation while the operation is in progress, respectively.

> TIP: Transform about your 3D objects' axes instead of your pages' axes by holding the **Ctrl** key down as you transform.

You can also adjust the angle and elevation of each "active" light on the page by dragging the light pointer to a position which simulates a light source.

> After any transformation, the underlying base object remains editable.

To add dimensionality:

1. Select an object and click the [icon] **Instant 3D** button on the Drawing toolbar.

    The object immediately adopts 3D characteristics with a blue orbit circle displayed in the object's foreground. You'll also notice a 3D-specific context toolbar appear above your drawing.

2. Click a 3D effect category from the first drop-down menu on the 3D context toolbar (from **Bevel**, **Lights**, **Lathe**, **Texture**, **Viewport**, **Material**); the other toolbars' options change dynamically according to the category currently selected. See DrawPlus Help for more details.

3. Set each drop-down menu or input box for each category in turn. A little experimentation is advisable.

4. Hover over the object's blue orbit circle and rotate about the X, Y or Z axis (or X and Y axes together) by dragging about the circle's periphery (depending on the currently displayed cursor).

If you're not happy with how your 3D object is looking, you can revert to the object's initial transformation by clicking the **Reset Defaults** button on the context toolbar.

To switch off 3D effects:

*   Click the **Remove Instant 3D** button on the context toolbar. You can always click the Drawing toolbar's **Instant 3D** button at any time later to reinstate the effect.

The Bevel and Lathe categories offer several presets that you can apply as your profile. You can also define your own custom profiles for both bevel and lathe effects from the Instant 3D context toolbar. (See DrawPlus help for more details.)

Pseudo 3D

Pseudo 3D produces an object **projection** to follow one of three separate planes (top, front or right), either by using an **Isometric projection** (default) or other more complex projection. By bringing together transformed objects on each plane you produce the illusion of working in three dimensions, from a simple cube (below) to more complex 3D shapes, text, etc.

Each projection, from the same Quick Square object, can be presented as follows (with a combined multi-object cube).

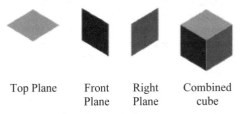

| Top Plane | Front Plane | Right Plane | Combined cube |

In DrawPlus, you can specify a plane (Top, Front, or Right) directly from the **Projection toolbar**. While working with this toolbar all newly created objects will be drawn according to the currently set plane. Only one plane can be set at any one time.

For more complicated projections, DrawPlus also allows **Cabinet Oblique**, **Cavalier Oblique**, and various **Dimetric** and **Trimetric** projections to be applied; you can also design your own **Custom** projection. All projections represent a different object position about the X, Y and Z axes. Here are some simple cubes to illustrate a simple isometric projection compared to some more advanced projections.

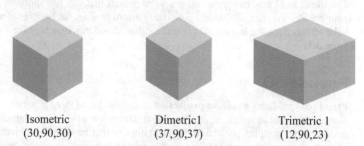

Isometric	Dimetric1	Trimetric 1
(30,90,30)	(37,90,37)	(12,90,23)

Notice how the displayed angles on each of the above projections are shown after each name.

Practically, projection drawing can be challenging as it's sometimes difficult to visualize objects that appear three dimensional. To aid drawing, you can call on the **snapping grid** which, when enabled, shows an alignment grid in the page background which intelligently switches to the current plane that you're working on. Whichever plane is set, drawn objects will then snap to the grid on the same plane.

To apply a Pseudo 3D projection:

1. From the Projection toolbar, select the **Top Plane**, **Front Plane**, or **Right Plane** button to set the plane to work on. (You'll see the **snapping grid** appear which reflects the currently set plane.)

2. Click a drawing tool and drag out the object (e.g., a Quick Rectangle) on the plane (an isometric projection is created by default).

3. All subsequently drawn objects are projected onto the currently set plane, unless it is swapped to a different plane (select a different button and draw a new object).

If this step-by-step process is followed, it's possible to bring together projected objects to create a larger object which simulates 3D characteristics.

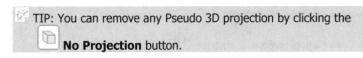

TIP: You can remove any Pseudo 3D projection by clicking the **No Projection** button.

The Switch Plane on Select button, when enabled, swaps the plane to that of a selected object (whether projected or not). If disabled, object selection will no longer automatically switch plane.

If you're creating a large number of objects, all on different planes, you can select all objects which project onto the same plane—useful for changing the colour of object faces for instance.

Selecting objects on the same plane:

- From the **Select All On Plane** option on the Edit menu, choose **None**, **Top**, **Front**, or **Right** from the menu.

To project an object to a different plane:

- Select a previously projected object, and with the **Ctrl** key depressed, choose a different plane's button from the Projection toolbar.

Using Advanced Pseudo 3D

Up to now we've assumed that you've applied a default isometric projection. However, DrawPlus can create other axonometric projections by changing the current projection properties.

To apply an advanced Pseudo 3D projection:

1. Select the object.

2. Click the **Projection Properties** button.

3. From the **Projection Properties** dialog, select a projection type from the first drop-down list. You'll notice the X, Y and Z axis values update to reflect the currently set projection.

Creating a custom projection:

- From the **Projection Properties** dialog, select **Custom** as the projection name from the first drop-down menu.
  OR

- Pick a preset projection instead, and modify **Angle** and/or **Scale** values for any axis. The projection's name changes to **Custom**.

Saving a custom projection:

1. For a Custom projection, click the 💾 **Save** button.

2. In the dialog enter a name for the new projection, and click **OK**. The entry will appear at the end of the drop-down menu.

12

Exporting and Publishing

Exporting objects and drawings

When you save a drawing, DrawPlus uses its own proprietary formats (.DPP for drawings, .DPX for templates and .DPA for animations) to store the information. From these formats it is possible to export your drawing as a graphic or simply print the drawing directly to a PDF file for electronic delivery/professional printing.

- **Export as graphics**: To be able to read the drawing into another application or use it on a Web page, the file needs to be saved in a suitable graphics format such as GIF, JPG or PNG. You can do this at any time using **Export>Export as Image...** on the File menu or via **Dynamic Preview**. The former displays the powerful Export Optimizer, which lets you preview how your document will look in any available format and choose to export one or more selected objects; the latter allows editing during preview—great for pixel-accurate editing of your intended output. For the former option, before making up your mind, you can even compare side-by-side views using different export settings. For converting DrawPlus objects into pictures on the page, the **Tools>Convert to Bitmap...** command can be used.

- **Printing**: DrawPlus provides versatile printing capabilities to handle a range of document types, including multi-page documents; large-format posters and banners, folded documents such as cards or brochures, and various sheet and label formats. You can do both spot colour and process colour separations and set a wide range of prepress options for professional printing. And whether you're delivering work to a printer or sharing it over the Web, you can save a tree or two by publishing directly to the Adobe PDF format.

  See **Basic Printing** on p. 245 for more information.

For details on exporting animations, see **Exporting animations** on p. 206.

Export optimizer

Especially if you're exporting Web bitmap images, you can take advantage of the **Export Optimizer**, which will greatly help you in reducing file sizes and download times as far as possible while maintaining image quality.

The Export Optimizer consists of a left-hand options region and a right-hand preview display, with additional buttons along the bottom of the dialog. Two tabs appear in Drawing Mode, and a third for Stopframe animation export only.

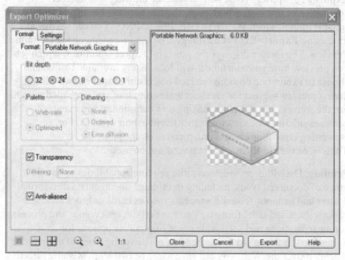

To export via the Export Optimizer:

1. Choose **Export>Export as Image...** from the File menu.

2. From the **Format** tab, select a graphics file type from the **Format** drop-down menu. The tab will display different options depending on the chosen graphics format. Change settings as appropriate to the file format selected (see DrawPlus help for more information).

3. (Optional) From the **Settings** tab, you can scale the image to a new size if desired (change **Pixels**), or adjust the **dpi** (dots per inch) setting. For graphics to be used on-screen, it's best to leave these values intact. The export can be based on the **Whole Page**, **Selected Region**, or **Selected Objects**. You can uncheck **Image Slices** or **Hotspots** if you've create these elements but don't want them exported.

4. Click the **Export** button. If you click **Close**, DrawPlus remembers your preferred format and settings, particularly useful for adjusting the setting which are used if you preview the image in a browser (using **File>Preview in Browser**).

Dynamic preview

Although the Export Optimizer's preview options lets you see how your export will look, it's time-consuming to repeatedly export your graphic until you get the output exactly as you want it. Instead, you can use **Dynamic Preview**, which lets you swap to a **preview-and-edit** mode, showing how your graphics will export directly on the page. It also lets you edit that output while still previewing, and set up the exported file's name, format and other settings. The ability to fine-tune object positioning to pixel level gives an added advantage for Web graphics developers.

Firstly, you'll need to configure your **Preview Settings...** such as file format, size and resolution (DPI) in advance of previewing. Secondly, you can use **Export Preview As...** to save to a filename. Finally, you can toggle between normal mode and Dynamic Preview mode at any time for on-the-page previewing and editing. Remember to perform repeated saves with the **Export Preview As...** option.

To change export settings:

1. Either:

   - From the Hintline toolbar, click the down arrow on the **Dynamic Preview** button, and choose **Preview Settings...**. The option launches a dialog, which closely resembles the Export Optimizer dialog (see above).
     OR

   - From **View Quality** on the View menu, choose **Preview Settings...**.

2. Change settings on the **Format** and **Settings** tab. Settings on the Format tab change according to file type (see DrawPlus help for more information).

3. Click **OK**.

To export via Dynamic Preview:

1. Select **Export Preview As...** from either the down arrow on the **Dynamic Preview** button (Hintline toolbar) or via **View>View Quality...**.

2. From the dialog, you'll be prompted for a file name to which you can save your graphic. Choose a folder location and enter a file name.

To toggle between Normal and Preview Mode:

- Click the **Dynamic Preview** button on the Hintline toolbar (or equivalent from **View>View Quality...**). If you've multiple documents loaded, you'll notice the current document's tab at the top of your workspace indicate the change to preview mode, e.g.

Drawing2

    To revert to Normal mode, click the button again.

While in this mode, any object can be manipulated or modified as if you are working in normal drawing mode, but what you're seeing is an accurate portrayal of your graphic to be exported.

Previewing the printed page

The **Print Preview** button changes the screen view to display your layout without guides, rulers, and other screen items. Special options, such as tiled output or crop marks, are displayed.

To preview the printed page:

- Click the **Print Preview** button on the Standard toolbar.

In Print Preview mode, the lower toolbar provides a variety of familiar view options (from left to right): Zoom percent, Zoom Out, Zoom slider, Zoom In, the Zoom (region) Tool, Actual Size, and Fit Page.

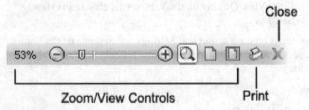

To cancel Print Preview mode:

- Click the **Close** button.

Basic printing

DrawPlus supports printing directly to a physical printer (e.g., All-in-ones, Inkjet and Laser printers) or to an electronic file such as Adobe Acrobat PDF. The printing feature allows scaling, tiling, and many other useful printing options for either method.

For the moment we'll look at basic printing to "real" printers. However, if you're working with a service bureau or commercial printer and need to provide PDF output, see **Publishing as PDF** on p. 248.

To set up your printer or begin printing:

- Click the ⬙ **Print** button on the Standard toolbar.
  OR

- Choose **Print...** from the File menu, or after right-clicking on the page or pasteboard.

The Print dialog appears.

To print:

1. On the **General** tab, select a printer from the list. If necessary, click the **Properties** button to set up the printer for the correct page size, etc. Set the page size from the **Advanced** button. Depending on your printer driver, to print text with shading or custom settings, enable the option to "Send True Type as Bitmap" option.

2. If necessary, click the **Layout** to set options for scaling, thumbnails, multiple pages, or tiling. For details, see **Printing special formats** (on p. 246).

3. Select the print range to be printed—choose the whole document, current page, selected pages/page ranges as options.

4. Select the number of copies.

5. If required, save the current settings to a Print profile (see below).

6. Click **OK**.

The Preview window shows how your document maps to the selected paper size.

The pages will be printed in colour on a colour printer or in shades of grey on a black and white printer.

You can save the current combination of settings made in the Print dialog as a print profile with a unique name. Note that the profile includes settings from all tabs except the Separations tab. (By the way, don't confuse these DrawPlus "print profiles" with ICC "device profiles.").

To save current print settings as a print profile:

1. On the Print dialog's **General** tab, click the **Save As...** button next to the Print Profile list.

2. Type in a new name and click **OK**.

The settings are saved as a file with the extension .PPR.

You can restore the profile later on simply by choosing its name in the list.

Printing special formats

In Normal drawing mode, using the DrawPlus **Page Setup** and printing options, you can set up pages for a variety of document types, such as Special Folded documents (greetings cards), Large documents (posters and banners), and Small documents (business cards, labels, tags). The Print dialog's **Layout** tab lets you specify other printing options, including scaling, thumbnails, multiple pages, and tiling..

Folded documents

DrawPlus automatically performs **imposition** of folded documents (cards, menus, etc.) when you use the Startup Wizard or **File>Page Setup...** to define a "Special Folded" document type. The settings ensure that two, three or four pages of the document are printed on each sheet of paper, with pages printed following the document sequence. This saves you from having to calculate how to position and collate pairs of pages on a single larger page, and lets you use automatic page numbering for the various pages.

The types most appropriate to invitations and greetings cards, include Tent Card, and Side/Top Fold Menu, Top Fold-Quarter size, Tri-Fold, or Z-Fold.

To produce double-sided sheets, check the **Balanced** option (for balanced margins) in Page Setup, then your printer's double-sided option or run sheets through twice, printing first the front and then the back of the sheet (reverse top and bottom between runs).

Printing posters and banners

Posters and banners are large-format documents where the page size extends across multiple sheets of paper. To have DrawPlus take care of the printing, set up your document beforehand using **File>Page Setup...** (with the "Large" document type option) to preview and select a particular preset arrangement (e.g., choose orientation).

Even if the document isn't set up as a poster or banner, you can use tiling and scaling settings (see below) to print onto multiple sheets from a standard size page. Each section or tile is printed on a single sheet of paper, and the various tiles can then be joined to form the complete page. To simplify arrangement of the tiles and to allow for printer margins, you can specify an overlap value.

To print a poster or banner from a standard size page:

1. First create your standard sized page (e.g., A4).

2. On the Print dialog's **Layout** tab, check the "Print tiled pages" option for overlapped multiple sheets, and set the "% Scale factor" to print at a larger size (e.g. 300%).

Printing business cards and labels

While DrawPlus can deal with large-format documents it is equally suited to documents where the design can be repeated multiple times on the same page during printing. Set up your drawing beforehand using **File>Page Setup...** (with the "Small" document type option) to preview and select a particular preset arrangement.

At print time, you can set the "Multiple pages per sheet" option to **Repeat pages to fill sheet**, **Each page N times** or **Full sheet of each page** in the **Print>Layout tab**. You can tell DrawPlus to skip a certain number of regions on the first sheet of paper—useful if, for example, you've already peeled off several labels from a label sheet, and don't want to print on the peeled-off sections.

> If you haven't set up the drawing as a Small Drawing, but still want to print multiple pages per sheet, try using the **Fit Many** option.

Printing thumbnails

*   Under "Special Printing" on the Print dialog's **Layout** tab, set the "Print as thumbnails" option to print multiple pages at a reduced size on each printed sheet, taking printer margins into account. Specify the number of thumbnails per sheet in the value box.

DrawPlus will print each page of the document at a reduced size, with the specified number of small pages or "thumbnails" neatly positioned on each printed sheet.

Publishing as PDF

PDF (short for Portable Document Format) is a cross-platform file format developed by Adobe to handle documents in a device- and platform-independent manner. In a relatively short time, PDF has evolved into a worldwide standard for document distribution which works equally well for electronic or paper publishing.

Although PDF excels as an electronic distribution medium it is also an excellent format for delivering a drawing file to a professional printer. In recent years, print stores are moving away from PostScript and toward the newer, more reliable PDF/X formats expressly targeted for graphic arts and high quality reproduction. Your print partner can tell you whether to deliver PDF/X-1 or PDF/X-1a (DrawPlus supports both)—but from the DrawPlus end of things you won't see a difference. In either mode, all your drawing's colours will be output in the CMYK colour space, and fonts you've used will be embedded. A single PDF/X file will contain all the necessary information (fonts, images, graphics, and text) your print partner requires to generate either spot or process colour separations.

If professional printing is required, you'll need to select Prepress options (via the Print dialog's **Prepress** tab) before choosing to output your drawing.

To export your document as a PDF file:

1. Prepare the document following standard print publishing guidelines, and taking the distribution method into account.

2. (Optional) To create pop-up annotations, insert PageHints as needed.

3. Choose **Publish as PDF...** from the File menu and check your export settings. (To export the whole document using default settings, you won't need to change any settings.) Make further last-minute changes (for example, a custom setting required by your print bureau).

4. Review General, Prepress, Compression, Security, and Advanced tab settings (see DrawPlus Help for more details).

   When preparing a PDF/X file for professional printing, choose either "PDF X/1" or "PDF X/1a" in the General tab's Compatibility drop-down list, as advised by your print partner. Also enquire whether or not to **Impose pages**; this option is fine for desktop printing of a folded drawing or one that uses facing pages, but a professional printer may prefer you to leave the imposition (page sequencing) to them.

5. Click **OK** to proceed to export.

If you checked **Preview PDF file in Acrobat**, the resulting PDF file appears in the version of Acrobat Reader installed on your system.

Exporting to CAD/CAM

DrawPlus allows your drawing to be exported as .DWG or .DXF, which lets you open your drawing in a number of AutoCAD program versions (namely AutoCAD R12, 2000 or 2004). The DWG file format is the native format for AutoCAD; drawings are created and saved in this format. The DXF format is an AutoCAD interchange format (ASCII) which can be read by almost all CAD products on personal computers, i.e. non-AutoCAD systems. If the intended export is for owners of AutoCAD itself, it is best to choose the .DWG format.

Export to DWG or DXF

The process by which you can export to DWG or DXF is much the same—you select a file format for export and the resulting dialog (identical for either format) lets you select a specific page and AutoCAD format for export, amongst other options.

To export as a DWG or DXF file:

1. Create your DrawPlus drawing.

2. Click Export>Export for CAD/CAM... on the File menu.

3. In the dialog, you will be asked for a file name and type (DWG, DXF, PLT)—choose a file location and a type of either DWG or DXF (see above). Click the **Save** button.

4. The resulting **Export DWG** dialog will appear allowing you to alter some settings.

    - You can decide which **Page** you would like to export.

    - Pick a **Format** which matches the version of AutoCAD used by your intended audience.

    - Check **Convert Text To Vector** to export all text as lines.

    - Check **Ignore Line Width** to export all lines with zero width.

    - Check **Monochrome** to ignore all colour settings and export everything as Black/White.

5. Click **OK** to export.

Export to HPGL

It is possible to export to HPGL (.PLT file format) for certain plotters and cutters.

The PLT file format does not contain colour information. Instead, the various objects in a PLT file have certain pen numbers associated with them. When exported, each pen number is assigned a specific colour. You can specify the colour assigned to a particular pen, so that you can match the original colours of the graphic.

A Pen selection list contains 256 pens although not all of the pens may be assigned (in fact you may use only a few). You can change the colour assignments by choosing the pen and then choosing a new colour for that pen, and even save the pen assignment to a library file for future use.

To export as an HPGL PLT file:

1. Create your DrawPlus drawing.

2. Click **Export for CAD/CAM...** on the File menu.

3. In the dialog, you will be asked for a file name and type—choose a file location, pick **HPGL Files (*.plt)** and enter a file name. Click the **Save** button.

4. The resulting **Export HPGL** dialog will appear allowing you to set export settings under the **Pens** and **Page** tabs.

5. In the Pens tab you can:

   - Change the pen colour assignment by selecting a pen in the pen list and then picking a new colour from the **Pen Colour** list box. Choosing "(Custom)" brings up a colour definition dialog box that allows you to define a custom colour using RGB values.

   - If needed, change the pen width assignments by choosing a new width for a selected pen from the **Pen Width** list box.

   - If needed, change the pen velocity by choosing a new velocity for that selected from the **Pen Velocity** list box.

   - If you want to unassign a pen, click the **Pen Unused** button.

   - You can also reset the current Pen Library pen settings to the previously saved settings.

6. If you've altered pen assignments, click the **Save** button to store your new settings. The changes are stored in the (Default) library.

7. In the Page tab you can pick page-related settings:

    *   You can decide which **Page** you would like to export.

    *   Set the Plotter Units.

    *   Define the **Plotter Origin** as being Page Centre or Bottom Left.

    *   The **Curve Resolution** can be set to a value between 0.0 and 1.0 inches (centimetres and millimeters can also be used as units). The value can be very precise; up to four decimal places are accepted. A setting of 0.0 results in the highest resolution, but it also greatly increases file size. A curve resolution of 0.016 inches is recommended.

8. Click **OK** to export.

> When outputting, the Pen with the closest matching colour will be chosen. If more than one Pen is defined with the same colour the Pen with the closest width will be chosen.

Notes

*   Bézier curves are converted to line segments.

*   Outline thickness and calligraphic settings are lost.

Saving your Pen Assignment Library

*   If you've modified your pen assignments and you want to create a separate library file, you can enter a new library name in the **Pen Library** list box and click the **Save** button. The pen library can then be selected from the drop-down list. To remove it, select it from the list and click the **Delete** button.

13

Index

Notes

Notes

Notes

Notes

Notes

Notes